DIVINE INTERVENTION:

A STORY OF HEALING, LOVE, AND HOPE

TERENCE ANGTUACO, M.D.

authorHOUSE®

AuthorHouse™
1663 Liberty Drive
Bloomington, IN 47403
www.authorhouse.com
Phone: 833-262-8899

Published by AuthorHouse 03/30/2023

ISBN: 979-8-8230-0370-4 (sc)
ISBN: 979-8-8230-0369-8 (e)

I dedicate this book to my wife, Josephine,
and to our three children, Tyler, Julienne,
and Jaymie. This book is a testament of their
selflessness, courage, and strength.

Thank you to everyone who helped us and encouraged
us through the most difficult time of our lives. Thank
you also to those who helped make this book a reality.

TABLE OF CONTENTS

PROLOGUE

This book is about God's love, mercy, power, and faithfulness. It is my wish that you will find hope, encouragement, and comfort in my testimony. I pray that after reading this book, you will be willing to trust God for everything. Hopefully, you will come to the conclusion that trusting Him is the wisest thing to do, the safest road to take, and always your best option.

"I cried to you for help, O Lord my God, and you healed me; you kept me from the grave. I was on my way to the depths below, but you restored my life. Sing praise to the Lord, all his faithful people! Remember what the Holy One has done and give him thanks! His anger lasts only a moment, his goodness for a lifetime. Tears may flow in the night, but joy comes in the morning. You have changed my sadness into a joyful dance; you have taken

away my sorrow and surrounded me with joy. So I will not be silent; I will sing praise to you. Lord, you are my God; I will give you thanks forever." (Psalm 30:2-5,11-12 GNTD)

Chapter 1

How It All Began

"You MUST call Father Ralph tonight at 7 p.m.!"

This was the voicemail message on our home phone from Sister Mary, a nun friend of ours, who had been ministering to us and helping pray for Jaymie's healing. Her voice had this uncontainable excitement.

Jaymie is our youngest daughter, who at the age of five, was diagnosed with a rare blood disorder that shut down her bone marrow. She became dependent on blood transfusions to keep her alive. This life-changing event came without any warning. There was no time to prepare us for what was about to come.

We came to know Sister Mary through her niece, who lived in our neighborhood. She is a nun from

Corpus Christi, Texas, whom we had met a few times when she came to visit her niece in Little Rock, Arkansas. There was an instant bond between us the first time we met. Before long, we became like family to each other.

One day, Sister Mary met this "healing priest" from Rockport, Texas, named Father Ralph Jones. He is well-known for having helped bring healing to many sick people through his prayers. Sister Mary had been tirelessly praying for Jaymie's healing, and her unexpected meeting with Father Ralph must have been an answer to her prayers. She talked to him about Jaymie's condition, and he graciously offered to help pray for her. Since we were not able to go to his chapel in Rockport, he said he would pray over Jaymie via the telephone. Sister Mary reminded me repeatedly on her voicemail message that day, that I must call Father Ralph at 7 p.m.

Indeed, that was the most important phone call I had made in my life. One that would change my life forever.

Chapter 2
The Anointing

There was a time when Jaymie required platelet transfusion every two to three days. Whenever her platelet count dropped below 20,000, she would bleed spontaneously, usually from her nose. It could certainly be much worse than that. But I knew that Jaymie was special in God's eyes, and somehow, I believed that things would be alright.

One Saturday afternoon, Jaymie's nose started bleeding and would not stop. It had been two days since her last platelet transfusion. We knew that her platelet count must have dropped, and she would need to be transfused quickly. We rushed her to the emergency room, with our two other children in tow.

We waited patiently for Jaymie to get through her platelet transfusion. The kids kept themselves entertained by watching television, while my wife and I prayed, encouraged each other, and kept our minds focused on only positive thoughts. In order to survive this stressful situation, we had to stay disciplined and not allow panic and despair to take root in our minds.

We were in the emergency room for a long time. While I sat mindlessly watching the minutes pass, I suddenly realized that it was 7 p.m., and I MUST call Father Ralph.

He picked up the phone right away. For some reason, I felt relieved. I introduced myself and told him that Sister Mary had asked me to call. We exchanged pleasantries, and he proceeded to ask about Jaymie. I told him that we were in the emergency room because Jaymie had bled and needed a platelet transfusion. His voice was kind and sincere. I felt comforted. I felt that he understood our pain. I felt that he truly cared. I felt like I was somehow talking to God.

He quoted me many scripture verses as he tried to comfort me and give me courage. Coincidentally, they were the exact verses that God placed in my heart when I prayed for comfort, strength, and direction. Furthermore, he also told me that I would be writing a book, not for financial gain, but purely for the glory of God. It felt surreal. He left me in a state of awe and amazement for I had just told my wife about that exact plan just a few hours prior. How can this man whom I have never met know about my private conversations with God and my wife? I felt like I had just talked to God, but this time, I heard an audible voice.

Father Ralph told me that God was using Jaymie's illness to prepare me to heal the sick. He had never asked me what I do for a living. I stretched out my right hand as he had instructed. He asked me to make the sign of the cross on my right hand using my left, as he prayed and "anointed" me to heal the sick in God's name. He then asked me to put my right hand on Jaymie's head as he said a prayer for her healing. What followed was a supernatural experience. There was a warmth that extended from my right shoulder down to my right hand. My heart was burning. I felt like something special was happening. After all this, I had to sit down as I felt drained.

It was not clear to me whether Father Ralph knew that I am a doctor when he said that God was preparing me to heal the sick. So, I told him, "Father, I am a doctor." To which he said, "Is that so?" It was then that I understood that the healing God was preparing me to do was the kind that is beyond giving medicines or cutting out tumors.

When all this sunk in, I felt nervous, insecure, and confused. I asked God, "Why me?" "What am I supposed to do?" I argued with God that I could not do this, that I had no training or experience in it, and that I was simply, not the right choice. God may be perfect and all-knowing, but not this time. I became very anxious until I realized, well, there was nothing I needed to do about this anointing thing at this time, anyway. So, I decided to just relax for the time being. Besides, I had a lot on my plate caring for Jaymie.

A few weeks later, during one of Jaymie's frequent re-hospitalizations, I found myself in the family room of the Hematology and Oncology ward trying to unwind from a stressful and exhausting day. Jaymie had just been admitted to the room after more than five hours of waiting in the Emergency department. It was 2 a.m. and I was flipping through television channels, hoping to watch a replay of the 2012 London Olympics. What I did not expect to see at that time was my favorite television preacher, Joel Osteen. His face occupied the entire television screen, and with his forefinger pointing at me, he commanded, "Those of you who had been anointed, do not be afraid. Pull your shoulders back and keep your chin up."

I almost fell off my chair.

Joel Osteen went on to remind his viewers how Moses felt inadequate and insecure when God gave him the mission to lead the Israelites out of Egypt. Moses argued that he was not eloquent enough, and God said that He would put the words in his mouth and tell him what to say. Moses then worried that people might not believe that his message came from God. So, God gave him the power to show signs to prove this. God asked him to throw his staff on the ground and it became a snake. He asked Moses to pick up the snake by its tail, and it became a staff.

I did not fall off my chair, but I did fall on my knees and prayed "Lord Jesus, I will do what you have asked me to do."

Chapter 3

Flashback: Freefall

About ten years prior, at the age of forty-three, I was at the pinnacle of my success, so to speak. My life was in many ways, perfect, or at least, I thought it was. I felt I deserved it because I had persevered and worked very hard to get there. Despite being told during medical residency training by my assistant program director that she did not think I would be able to gain acceptance to a fellowship training position in Gastroenterology, I did make it, and I became a pretty successful gastroenterologist. Financially, I was secure and stable. I also enjoyed a happy family life with a beautiful and loving wife, Josephine, and three amazing kids. We were all happy and healthy. There was nothing more I could ask. As a bonus, I even earned a national title in taekwondo. Not bad for a nerd in high school whom no one, including myself, believed for a second could excel in sports.

I was caring and sensitive to the needs of others, but I rarely went out of my comfort zone to reach out to those who were in need. I just wanted to mind my own business and keep my happy life undisturbed. It was as if my sole obligation in life was to my family. I lived a very disciplined life, but over time, I became more lax. It was as if all those years of hard work and the success that resulted, justified my behavior. Slowly, I became more free-spirited and probably, careless in my thoughts, words, and actions. I prayed regularly, but I never really dedicated time exclusively to know, feel, and communicate with God. With my life the way it was, I did not feel there was anything I needed or wanted to change at that time.

During the spring break of 2012, we decided to go on a family skiing trip to Colorado. We stayed at a luxurious resort, and everyone had a great time. We pampered ourselves and felt that we deserved it. The kids were excited about learning how to ski. The scenery from the mountaintop was breathtaking. My wife and I enjoyed watching the kids have a great time. It was a perfect vacation, except, on the last two days of our stay, I woke up earlier than usual because I had this unexplainable and indescribable feeling of discomfort, even disgust. So much so that I told my wife about it several times.

The day after we got home, the kids went back to school. Jaymie had some nose bleeds in school and the teacher told my wife about it when she picked her up after school. We thought the dry air in Colorado may have contributed to this. She had a few more episodes at home, so I thought I would get some silver nitrate sticks from my clinic the next day and cauterize her nose if I could identify the source of bleeding. Somehow, something made me uncomfortable with the thought of doing this. I decided to call my colleague and friend who is an ear, nose, and throat (ENT) specialist. He was kind enough to work Jaymie in to check her nose the next morning. He cauterized her nose where he thought the bleeding came from and Jaymie went back to school after that. A few hours later, the teacher called my wife because Jaymie's nose started bleeding again, and even more profusely. My wife picked her up from school and brought her to my clinic to get a complete blood count (CBC) test to see if she had become anemic from all this blood loss. Since her nose bleeding had stopped, my wife brought her back to school after the blood draw. We were not expecting anything to be wrong with her blood test and did not wait for the results. After about an hour, the laboratory called me with the result. To my surprise and shock, Jaymie's platelet count was extremely low at 5,000. Platelets are blood cells that plug up bleeding vessels to prevent or stop bleeding. The normal level is 150,000 and spontaneous bleeding can occur if it goes below 20,000. I called my wife with the results. She had just dropped off Jaymie at school. We pulled her out of school again and brought her back to my clinic to repeat the blood test. We thought the results could not be correct. It must have been a laboratory error. At least, that was what we wished and wanted to believe. Besides, we have a perfect life and things like this do not happen to people like us. The repeat blood test confirmed that the value was correct, and this time, the platelet count was even lower at 3,000.

I called a friend and colleague who is an adult blood specialist (hematologist). He advised us to consult a pediatric hematologist right away. Being the friend that he is, he helped make phone calls to get Jaymie the medical care she needed, as soon as possible. I did not know a pediatric hematologist, and our panicked state of mind distracted us from what we needed to do at that time.

Luckily, we got to see someone that day at the Arkansas Children's Hospital. The doctor drew some blood and looked at it under the microscope. She concluded that this was a condition called ITP (idiopathic thrombocytopenic purpura). Jaymie would have to be admitted and given intravenous immunoglobulins, and her platelets should rise back up within 24 hours. We were relieved and very grateful to the doctor. Who would not welcome a favorable doctor's report? Other than childbirth, this was the first time an immediate family member of ours had to be hospitalized.

We were anxious, yet optimistic and excited, as we anticipated hearing some good news the next day. Much to our chagrin, Jaymie's platelet count did not go up as expected, and instead, decreased further. The diagnosis was most likely incorrect. She got her first of many blood transfusions on that day, and we were devastated. My wife is a pediatrician, and we both knew this was not good. The reality of the situation hit us hard. We went through a myriad of emotions, from disbelief, to anger, helplessness, and despair. We had hit rock bottom.

Chapter 4

Broken

The first of hundreds of blood transfusions started flowing through Jaymie's veins. The first of thousands of needle sticks for blood draws, the first of hundreds of days in the hospital, the first of countless teardrops, and the first of endless restless days and sleepless nights had just begun.

Every two to three days, Jaymie would require platelet transfusions. Her count would not rise above the danger level after transfusion, or it would drop back down quickly within a short period of time. Her doctor was a lovely man, and he tried his best to give us the information we needed and the hope we yearned for. Like us, he seemed to find it hard to accept that something terrible like this could happen to a family like ours. We would go over graphs and trends of Jaymie's blood test results, and he would try to find some nuances to their interpretation that might give us some hope that all will be well and that this would all go away soon. He offered plausible explanations for why her platelet count did not respond to the transfusions. Maybe the blood product was nearing the end of its shelf-life, or maybe there was some minor incompatibility with Jaymie's blood type. He did his job as a doctor. That is, if he could not cure, he would at least try to comfort. I knew what he was doing. I had done the same to my patients before. But we wanted hope, and we chose to believe him. More than that, we wanted a cure. And we wanted it ASAP.

After a week, there was no improvement. We wanted to deny there was a problem because we wanted to keep hoping. But because we wanted a cure, we needed to act. The doctor decided that it was necessary to perform a bone marrow biopsy. It was an invasive test. I had done one before on one of my patients when I was an intern. To this day, I can still remember the awful sensation of something crunching as I drilled that needle through my patient's hip bone many years ago. The sheer thought of my sweet little five-year-old baby girl going through this was just horrifying. We did not have a choice, though. It needed to be done.

The day of reckoning had arrived. My wife and I held hands and cried in private. We put on a brave face in front of Jaymie to give her the courage to face her battle. We made light of the situation to give her the distraction she needed to avoid feeling the mental anguish of this impending torture. She was old enough to understand things, and she wanted information. We only told her what she wanted to know. Unfortunately, she wanted to know more than what we thought she needed. At one point, she asked my wife point-blank, "Mommy, am I gonna die?" How does one answer that question? Why should any parent have to experience being asked that question? Who can continue to pretend to be brave and strong when faced with this situation? Not us. The dam broke, and our tears overflowed.

The bone marrow biopsy went well, and we received the results the following day. There was seventy percent cellularity of her bone marrow. Simply put, this means that although she incurred some damage, her bone marrow has enough cells to recover and produce blood cells again. That was great news. Maybe it was all going to be okay. Perhaps, this nightmare was going to end soon. The doctor thought that this could be due to an infection Jaymie got while we were in Colorado. He ordered a bunch of tests checking for virus infections and tick-borne illnesses. We hoped they would come back positive for one of them because they are treatable, and the damage could be reversible.

Days turned into weeks. Nothing changed in Jaymie's clinical condition. She was not improving and required platelet transfusions every two to three days.

The tests for viruses and tick-borne illnesses came back negative.

In academic centers, doctors rotate through different assignments and took turns running the hospital ward. Another doctor took over Jaymie's case. Dr. Robert Saylors, a senior staff member, reviewed Jaymie's test results. He was concerned that two cell lines were affected: the white blood cell (WBC) and the platelet. He was skeptical about the bone marrow biopsy findings and suspected that there might be a sampling error leading to a false-negative result. In other words, the bone marrow findings should be worse than what was reported, given Jaymie's clinical presentation. He asked for another bone marrow biopsy. We felt like we were back on this emotional roller coaster ride again. Our emotions vacillated between hope and hopelessness, relief and fear, and joy and despair. But we survived to tell our tale because no matter what the situation was at the time, there was always hope, there was always relief, and there was always joy.

Chapter 5
The Horrifying
Face of Reality

We struggled to find a way to tell Jaymie that she needed another bone marrow biopsy. My wife and I felt that it was important to tell her the truth. She needed to be able to trust us, as this was what would sustain her through this long and difficult ordeal. At five-years-old, Jaymie was old enough to remember and understand what happened the first time around. She knew that this repeat bone marrow biopsy would cause pain again. She would recall the horror of having a mask cover her face as they gave her the anesthetic to put her to sleep. She would be angry knowing that we would abandon her again as the doctors escort us out of the room before the procedure starts. In a situation like this, was there really a way to tell her what was about to happen without causing her fear and dread? There was none. And so, we told her the truth of what was about to happen, and we did our best to reassure and comfort her.

A few days later, the result of the repeat bone marrow biopsy came back. We sat down with Dr. Saylors who calmly told us that her bone marrow was "empty." There were no cells. This would explain why she was transfusion-dependent and required blood products every two to three days. Dr. Saylors thought that she likely had aplastic anemia. This is a dreadful disease where all three blood cell lines are affected. Jaymie's white blood cell count, red blood cell count, and platelet count were very low. Without blood, life is not sustainable. We were sustaining her through the kind and generous hearts of the many blood donors who sacrificed their own comforts to help save Jaymie's life.

It was a very sad and somber day. My heart felt like lead. I took deep breaths but the air I breathed in did not feel enough. I looked up at the beautiful morning sky and listened to the laughter around me, but I felt wretched and alone. There was nothing that could comfort me; nothing could give me any rest. I fell on my knees as I was so weak and broken. The only thing I had the strength to do was pray. I realized then that the one thing in life that required the least effort and gave the greatest consolation when it really mattered was prayer – pure, raw, and earnest prayer. In this state of awareness of my absolute dependence on God, I felt His presence, understood His love, and nothing else mattered.

CHAPTER 6

BUTTERFLIES: THE MESSAGES AND MESSENGERS FROM GOD

We have two other children, Tyler and Julienne. At the time of Jaymie's illness, they were ten and seven-years-old, respectively. They sacrificed and hurt just as my wife and I did. We left them with relatives or friends many times, when both of us had to be with Jaymie. They had to give up certain activities because we could not accompany them. We celebrated their birthdays that year in Jaymie's hospital room and there were no birthday candles to blow because we all had to wear masks. Jaymie's immune system was so weak because of her low white blood cell count that we had to protect her from our germs. Their lives were on hold. All of our lives, especially Jaymie's, were on hold.

One day, while Jaymie was still very ill, I had to go back home and check on our other two kids. They also needed me, just like Jaymie. I explained to them the gravity of Jaymie's condition. They did not seem to grasp the situation at the time. The three of us held hands and I prayed out loud. This was something I had never done before. Then, I started sobbing as I prayed. This was another thing I had never done before, especially in front of our kids. They were probably shocked and confused about what was going on, probably even wondered what was wrong with me. Tyler started cracking up. He later said that he did not know whether I was laughing or crying at the time and thought that I was just trying to be silly. Eventually, they understood the seriousness and grimness of the situation. I asked them for their understanding, cooperation, and support. And all these they happily gave. I am very proud of them for their maturity, generosity, and selflessness at such a young age.

I spent that night at home with them, while my wife stayed with Jaymie at the hospital. It was difficult for me to relax and fall asleep. The thought of my baby girl being sick in the hospital and away from me, kept me awake. I felt helpless as I had no control over the situation. Somehow, being near her gave me some sense of control and usefulness. If not for anything else, I could at least hug her, make her laugh, tell her stories, or simply lie quietly beside her and let her feel that I was there for her.

As I kept watch of the time and stressed about the dwindling number of hours left for me to sleep, I found myself talking to God. There was no one else to talk to at that time of the night. Even if there was, I did not feel that anyone could understand or soothe the pain I felt. The requests I made to God exposed the weakness of my faith. I needed Him to spoon-feed me baby food. I needed concrete answers from Him about Jaymie that I could see, and I wanted to be a hundred percent certain that they truly came from Him. Faith is believing in things we hope for even if we are not able to fathom how it can come to be. I did not have very much faith. God knew it, and I knew it. I was too weak to try to have more. I just needed God to show up, hold my hands, and lead me where I should go. To my surprise, this was exactly what He did.

I asked God to show me a sign to let me know that all would be well, and that Jaymie would eventually be cured of this illness. But I did not know what sign to ask for. I was too tired to think of something unique and unusual that would eliminate the likelihood of chance or coincidence. So, I said, "Lord, show me a sign. Anything. Maybe, a butterfly. Or maybe, tell me something in a dream. Anything. Anything." The next thing I knew, I fell asleep.

The next day, I brought Tyler and Julienne to the hospital to visit Jaymie. She missed them and needed some sense of normalcy. The two of them, on the other hand, were also eager to do something to cheer Jaymie up.

I was happy to find a nice parking spot and thanked the Lord, like I always do. I went around the passenger's side where Julienne was and opened the door for her. As she stepped out of the car, out of nowhere, a butterfly flew right between us, at our eye level. Julienne was amazed at how the butterfly just cut through right between us. At that time, I did not realize that this was the sign I had asked God for the night before. Then, as we were about to walk through the glass door entrance of the hospital building, another butterfly cut through in front of Tyler. Tyler wondered aloud where the butterfly came from as we were almost inside the building and away from any flowerbeds, plants, or trees. At that point, I suddenly realized that God had just answered my plea for a sign. I felt His presence. My chest felt tingly. My eyes watered. I could barely contain my excitement. I was sure that Jaymie would be cured.

That night, I slept well, and I had a very vivid dream. In that dream, someone handed me a piece of paper. It was a laboratory test report of someone's complete blood count (CBC). They were all normal. I did not see the face of the person holding the paper. But I remembered the hand and how it made me feel. I knew whose hand it was. I knew that Jaymie would be cured.

Chapter 7
No Match

So, it was decided that Jaymie would start on some toxic medications to treat what they thought at that time, was aplastic anemia. (This later turned out to be an incorrect diagnosis.) The treatment regimen consisted of some kind of horse serum and high dose steroids given intravenously, and an oral immune system suppressing agent called Cyclosporine that is commonly given to organ transplant patients. These drugs made her very sick. In the meantime, we had to be prepared for the worst-case scenario. If these medications did not work, Jaymie, who was five years old at that time, would need a bone marrow transplant. We were distraught having to deal with the uncertainties of the situation. Part of us wanted to go into denial to spare us from the pain and anxiety. But we had to be strong for our child. She needed us to fight for her so she would have a chance to survive.

It was necessary to first screen her siblings to see if they could be potential donors, as they were the ideal candidates. I wished that we, the parents, could be donors, but this was not the case. As it turned out, we faced a situation where we had to potentially expose another child to the risks of complications to save our sick child. We explained the screening procedure to Tyler and Julienne, which basically involved swabbing their mouths extensively to obtain enough cells for analysis. It would be uncomfortable, but not necessarily a painful procedure. The more challenging part of this was to explain to the kids what they would have to go through should one or both of them be found to be a compatible match for Jaymie as a donor. At that time, Tyler was ten years old and Julienne was seven, and they had to make an informed decision if they were willing to be a bone marrow donor for Jaymie. They knew how sick their baby sister was, and they understood that they could potentially save her life. But my wife and I wanted to make sure that they did not feel pressured to agree to this. We also needed to make sure that they would not feel the burden of guilt should they decide they did not want to do it or if they were deemed unsuitable candidates. We sought counselors to help us do this correctly. This was too important to mess up.

Tyler and Julienne were excited to go through the

donor screening process. Surprisingly, they only had a few questions. It seemed like they were just ready to do what was needed to help their baby sister. We felt like we over-prepared for this conference with the kids. We felt like we stressed over nothing. We told them what they needed to know and wanted to know. It was a lot easier and simpler than we anticipated. They were more mature than what we had given them credit for. The strength of their characters surprised us. We thought they were too young to handle big people matters such as this, but we were obviously wrong.

A few days later, we got the results of the screening test. Tyler and Julienne were a perfect match to each other, but neither of them was anywhere close to being a match with Jaymie. In other words, if Jaymie did not respond to the medicines she was getting, she would not be able to get a bone marrow transplant, unless we decide to do the riskier type of transplant using an unrelated donor. The search for an appropriately matched unrelated donor is a formidable task. We were devastated. We were worried and unsure of what the future might be like. We were terrified, and that was an understatement.

I left the hospital briefly to attend a school conference for Tyler's upcoming field trip. A parent of Tyler's classmate came up to me to ask how Jaymie was doing. As I attempted to answer her question, my lips quivered, my shoulders shook, and tears poured out uncontrollably. She had no idea how bad Jaymie's condition was, but they knew something was very wrong. I felt embarrassed and I was sure those people who saw me were just as embarrassed. Many of them, including the one who asked the question, walked away quietly. Their faces had the look of concern mixed with guilt for having caused my meltdown. None of them said a word, but their love was palpable. This moment was a gift of grace from God. At that moment, as I stood there by myself, God was with me. He held my hands as He had promised He would.

"For I am the LORD your God who takes hold of your right hand and says to you, do not fear; I will help you." (Isaiah 41:13 NIV)

Jaymie's friends and schoolmates found out about her plight. A few weeks later, they organized a bone marrow registry drive through Be The Match foundation. Family, friends and many people unknown to us came together and signed up to be potential bone marrow donors with the hopes of expanding the donor pool. This process would not only help Jaymie, should she need a bone marrow transplant, but it could also help countless other people around the world. In a sense, our suffering had served the greater purpose of helping lessen the sufferings of others.

CHAPTER 8
BORN AGAIN

Jaymie had not responded to the treatment regimen she had received thus far. She continued to require repeated blood and platelet transfusions every couple of days. The steroid treatment made her face swell and her back developed a hump. She was irritable and had difficulty sleeping at night. Jaymie was often tired, but she could not find rest. Her other medicine, Cyclosporine, made her grow excess hair on her face and back. She looked sick and was unrecognizable. The pain I felt whenever I looked at her was tough to bear. Cyclosporine also tasted so bad that no bribe of any kind of toys or candies could make her agree to take it. Even if she did, she would immediately throw it up. One time, the nurses asked my wife and me to step out of the room, and they literally tied her down and shoved the medicine down her throat. We stood outside the room and listened to her wail and shriek helplessly, like an animal on its way to the slaughterhouse. She desperately called out for us to come save her from the nurses. We did not because we could not. She needed the medicine. We felt useless and helpless. We felt like we abandoned her. I am sure she felt that way too.

For the next several weeks, Jaymie was in and out of the hospital, with more days in than out. Our bags were always packed and ready in case we had to rush her back to the hospital for an emergency. These emergencies were either due to bleeding or high fever. Whenever her platelets dropped below 20,000, she would have spontaneous nose bleeds, which could often be massive. One such time, she bled so much that her bedsheet was literally soaked in blood. Because the bleeding would not stop, despite our first-aid intervention, we had to call 911. Blood was gushing out of her nose like water from a faucet. We applied external pressure to her nose to try to stop the bleeding, but to no avail. Because of the brisk bleeding, she swallowed copious amount of blood which she would eventually vomit when her stomach filled up. It took forever for the ambulance to come help us. With the way she bled, they could not have arrived quickly enough. By the time she was attended to at the emergency room, Jaymie had lost half of her blood volume. It was a very frightening experience. After everything had settled down, the reality that we almost lost her struck us. It took me months to get over the trauma of that very eventful night. I could not keep myself from reliving those moments in my mind repeatedly. The sight of the huge pool of blood on our bed, the sound of our panicked voices, the metallic smell of the blood, and the thought of what could have been, lingered in my mind long after that night was over.

Because of her low white blood cell (WBC) count and the fact that she was taking medicines to suppress her immune system further, Jaymie was very susceptible to infections. To make matters worse, she had a long catheter, called a PICC line, placed in her vein that goes directly to her main blood vessel. This venous access was where blood products, medicines, and fluids were delivered, and blood samples were drawn from. These catheters are oftentimes a source of infection. Given her weakened immune system, the infection could spread to her blood quickly and make her very ill, called sepsis. Because of this, we were instructed to take her straight to the emergency room if she were to develop a fever. This happened quite frequently. The doctor would then admit her to the hospital, draw blood and send it for culture to determine what type of bacteria was present in her blood, start her on antibiotics, and if needed, change out the PICC line. This often required several days of hospitalization until she was deemed clear of infection and safe to return home. Unfortunately, we often did not get to stay home for very long, as these episodes of fever recurred quite frequently. After a while, we began to expect bad things to happen immediately following a brief reprieve. It became a never-ending cycle of "brief-relief" and "not-again". The "brief-relief" sometimes seemed like a heinous joke.

As if the bleeding and fever problems were not enough, Jaymie's liver enzymes were then found to be elevated. Initially, her doctor thought that this was likely due to her medications. They ran several tests which all returned negative. Over time, her liver enzymes continued to rise. During one of Jaymie's outpatient follow-up clinic visits, two days after being discharged from the hospital, her liver enzymes were so high that she had to be re-admitted immediately. She was given a few days of high-dose steroids, her liver enzymes improved, and she was sent home. It was a relief, albeit a brief one, because a few days later, she had a follow-up blood test at the outpatient clinic, and her liver enzymes were higher than they had ever been. She had to be readmitted to the hospital. Not again.

The doctor was perplexed and concerned about the degree of her liver test abnormality and her lack of response to the initial steroid treatment. He ordered a liver biopsy and consulted a liver specialist, who thought that Jaymie needed an even higher dose of steroid than what she had initially received.

I am an adult liver specialist, and I was well aware of what was involved in performing a liver biopsy. It was difficult for me to imagine the nightmare my five-year-old baby girl would have to go through. In the end, I was so thankful to God that the procedure went just fine without any complications, and Jaymie handled it really well. Furthermore, I was very grateful to have a very supportive family. My wife's sister and her husband stayed with us during the procedure as we waited anxiously for it to finish. Their sweet kids also came to visit Jaymie and encouraged her. They had been very helpful and supportive throughout this entire ordeal from the very beginning. They visited us at the hospital often, brought us warm restaurant food, and took care of our two other kids when my wife and I were both too busy and tied up taking care of our sick child in the hospital. Through our seemingly endless cycle of fear and agony, God often gave us relief through the warm experience of love from our family and friends. This gave us the strength to get up each day and continue to fight the battle that was ahead of us.

While waiting for the liver biopsy results, Jaymie resumed her steroid treatment but at a much higher dose. The amount she received was high, even for a large adult patient. This really affected her adversely. She would become extremely agitated with the slightest stimulation from bright light or loud sound. It also made her highly irritable, such that any change in her surroundings or situation would drive her up the wall. She would cry inconsolably, scream her lungs out, and kick everything within her reach even to the point of hurting herself. With her low platelet count, any trauma could potentially have dire consequences. My wife always knew what to do. She is a pediatrician by trade, but she has always been the perfect mother, knowing exactly what Jaymie needed at any given point in time. During these tantrum crises, the doctors would give her various medicines to calm her. These medicines, however, have side effects which made her feel worse. My wife thought it better to first try whatever non-pharmacological interventions at her disposal, rather than immediately ask the doctors for a shot. You will find out later in this chapter that among her options was asking me to leave the room.

Our kids were always very close to my wife and me. They were mommy's and daddy's boy and girls. As is the case with most girls to their dads, our girls also hold some special power over me, especially Jaymie. She sometimes believes that she has exclusive rights over me and will make it known to her mom, sister, and brother that they need to just wait for their turn. I have always enjoyed this privilege. However, during this time, while she was sick, I was the one she loved to hate. I did not mind this at all, but it did require some adjusting. Treating me like this probably gave her some sense of control in an otherwise out-of-control situation. At least I was useful to her in one way, shape, or form. I was happy just to be able to help make her feel better.

At one point during her treatment with very

high dose of steroid, she had one of her inconsolable tantrums. Even medications did not calm her down this time. Instead, they increased her agitation. This effect, called a "paradoxical response," is not uncommon with these mind-altering medications. My wife kept the environment dark and quiet, and asked me to step out of the room. For reasons unbeknownst to me, I was somehow contributing to Jaymie's agitation. My wife told me she would call me once Jaymie had settled down.

So, I sat outside the room and decided to pray the rosary. I went through five "decades" of it, but I could still hear Jaymie screaming through the closed door. My mind was restless, anxious, and worried, and I just wanted to feel God's presence. I needed to have some peace amid this chaos. Part of me sought an explanation, but the greater part of me wanted God to take this cup of suffering away from me. I opened the Bible app on my smartphone and randomly chose to read the book of Job. This was the first time I had ever read this. It was exactly what I needed. God must have heard my desperate pleas for help. After reading it in its entirety, Jaymie was still not ready for me to go back into the room. I decided to walk around the building to pass time and dull the pain in my chest. I stopped at the fourth floor to look out the window and enjoy the view of the newly built playground with the beautiful decorations of huge flowers surrounding it. The view somehow allured me, and my mind was lost in the moment. I must have been transported to this spiritual realm where I found myself having an intimate and deep conversation with God that required no words. I do recall asking God not to let my wife interrupt my conversation with Him, because I knew that at any time, she might call me and ask me to return to Jaymie's room. As I continued to stare mindlessly at the playground, I began to see my life flashing frame by frame before me, like a slide show. There were images of the times when I had sinned against God. As they were presented to me, I asked God for forgiveness. I do not know how long I stood there, but after it was all over, I felt sanctified, redeemed, and one with God. At that moment, I dedicated my life to serving God. I felt like I was born again. God had given me a new life. I found a new purpose in my existence. It felt like fire had descended upon me. I was energized and I was ready to take on a new mission.

I marked the date and time of this moment: June 16, 2012, at 5:55 p.m. This was the beginning of my new life.

As soon as my date with the Lord was over, my wife called and asked me to return to Jaymie's room. She was now calm and hungry, and wanted me to buy her some Kentucky Fried Chicken.

CHAPTER 9
ANOTHER FAILURE

My wife and I pushed Jaymie around the hospital in her stroller to keep her entertained and to distract our minds from the dire situation we were in. Whenever the gift shop was open, we would shop for toys. Otherwise, we would just shop for candies at the vending machines. Jaymie knew I liked the Payday peanut bars and she enjoyed buying them for me. Given that I had already involuntarily lost more than ten pounds at that point from all the stress, I was not worried about any weight gain from these unwanted calories.

As we took our daily strolls, we noticed that Jaymie's skin was turning more yellow each day. Her urine also turned darker and became tea colored. I knew that these were not good indicators. Her liver function tests were getting worse despite the very high doses of steroid she already received. I could tell that her liver was failing just by looking at her.

I received a call from the pathologist, who reviewed Jaymie's liver biopsy, as she was preparing to leave town. She was one of my former colleagues and she knew that I had been anxiously waiting for the results. The liver biopsy revealed the presence of some unusual cells called hemophagocytes, but according to her, they did not look overly concerning. The pathologist reassured me that the findings were, at worst, non-specific, and did not point to any specific diagnosis. She had already discussed the findings with Jaymie's physicians, and they decided there would be no change in the treatment plans.

Over the next few days, my level of anxiety went up exponentially. I was restless and unable to sleep. It might have been because, as a liver specialist, I knew that things had gone from bad to worse, and Jaymie was not responding to the treatment. On top of that, we did not have a clear diagnosis. Not only had her bone marrow failed, but her liver was on the verge of failing. My wife's sister, who is also a physician, insisted that my wife and I take some anti-anxiety medicine. She was worried that we were not resting, and it might begin to affect our own health. At first, we resisted, but after a few days, we agreed that we might actually need it. Given that we had never taken such medicines before, we were not sure how it might affect us. My wife thought it would be prudent for us to not take it at the same time, in case it affected our alertness and judgment, or make us sick. One of us needed to be always fully intact mentally to take care of Jaymie. We decided that I would take the anti-anxiety medicine first.

That night, I took the medicine as prescribed by my sister-in-law. My heart pounded and raced all night. I could not sleep or find a comfortable position. I felt jittery and easily startled. It could have been that my anxiety went overboard due to my exhaustion or from simply knowing that Jaymie's condition was continuing to worsen. It could certainly be the side effects of the medicine as well.

At around 5 a.m., I jumped out of bed and quickly went to the nurses' station to ask them if Jaymie's blood test results from that morning had returned. My intuition told me that something was gravely wrong. Unfortunately, the results were not back yet, and we had to wait patiently. It was not easy. While we waited, my wife and I analyzed Jaymie's test results and clinical condition. We reviewed the medical literature as best as we could. We recalled that Dr. Saylors had said earlier that it was unlikely that Jaymie had this condition called hemophagocytic lympho-histiocytosis or HLH, a rare disease causing the immune system to attack the bone marrow leading to bone marrow failure. It can also affect other organs including the liver and the brain.

She did not meet enough criteria required to make that diagnosis. Furthermore, she had not been as sick as those children with HLH usually are. Those patients are often critically ill and required admission to the intensive care unit (ICU). But we wondered about Jaymie's recurrent fever, her unexplained impending liver failure, and the fact that her bone marrow was not responding to the standard treatment for aplastic anemia. I also thought, "What if the presence of the non-specific cells called hemophagocytes that the pathologist saw on her liver biopsy was in fact a significant finding?" The possibility of HLH was always at the back of our minds. It's a fatal disease with limited treatment options. We did not want it and were still hoping that it was not what Jaymie had. However, I told my wife that if one of Jaymie's liver tests called bilirubin, returned higher than the previous day, we should request a transfer to Cincinnati Children's Hospital where they have expertise in treating HLH. This might give her a better chance of survival.

When the blood test results finally came, they confirmed my worst fears. Jaymie's bilirubin level had gone up to a level that was consistent with liver failure. She now had liver failure on top of her bone marrow failure.

If we were to go to Cincinnati for treatment, we needed to make plans to be there for several months and arrange for the care for our other two kids, who were only eight- and eleven-years-old at that time. It would be a challenge to get last-minute plane tickets, but more than that, we wondered if Jaymie was medically stable enough to travel. All of these issues and questions were overwhelming us at a time when we were already crushed over concerns about Jaymie's declining health. We reckoned that our lack of sleep, exhaustion, anxiety, and panic could possibly impair our judgment. Hence, I called my wife's sister and asked if she could come and help us with the important decisions we needed to make. She was kind enough to cancel her clinic at such short notice and rushed to the hospital to help us. In tough situations like this, God never failed to send us help. This was not the first time, and it would not be the last.

I asked the nurse to page Dr. Saylors and inform him of the blood test results and let him know we wanted to discuss his treatment plans as soon as possible. After he reviewed the results of Jaymie's recent tests, we discussed our concerns, and he gave us his opinion and recommendations.

Dr. Saylors wanted to start treating Jaymie for HLH as soon as possible, which was exactly what we were hoping he would say. At that point, there were more reasons to think she had HLH than not. He knew that we were considering a transfer to Cincinnati for further care, and he said he would respect our decision if that were the case. He reassured us though, that he had experience in treating this disease. This condition is very rare and occurs in about one in a million people. Worldwide experience in treating this condition is limited, at best. He explained the treatment protocol to us and made sure we understood the high risk of morbidity and mortality associated with the treatment itself. This was at least an eight-week course of chemotherapy with a very toxic drug, and Jaymie's condition was expected to get worse before it gets better. After eight weeks, the treatment plan would have to be determined based on her state of health at that time. Jaymie could become very, very ill with the treatment, but without it, there was no chance of surviving. If we decided to stay in Arkansas for treatment, Dr. Saylors promised that he will take personal care of Jaymie and make rounds on her every day, including weekends and holidays until her treatment is completed. We could not have asked for more than that.

At our moment of utmost vulnerability, we needed someone we could trust to help us through this mess. After our conference with Dr. Saylors, my wife and I did not feel we needed to go to Cincinnati. We trusted him. We were confident that Dr. Saylors would provide the best possible care that Jaymie needed.

The storm was sinking our boat. Although Jesus was with us, He remained asleep. Did He not know? Or did He just not care? We panicked and we woke Him up. It only took a word, and He calmed the storm. Then, we realized how little faith we had (In reference to Luke 8:22-25).

Chapter 10

The Paradox of Suffering

"*Blessed are you who are poor, for yours is the kingdom of God. Blessed are you who hunger now, for you will be satisfied. Blessed are you who weep now, for you will laugh.*" (Luke 6:20-21 NIV)

And so, the chemotherapy began. This would be a long and difficult journey. The doctor and his support staff prepared us for the worst by giving us an idea of what to expect. We were told that Jaymie would likely need another PICC line (central venous catheter) on her other arm. Not only did she dread the procedure itself, but she dreaded the weekly dressing changes. These catheters were secured and kept clean by a clear, sticky dressing that needed to be changed regularly to prevent infection. Because she continued to take Cyclosporine with her chemotherapy, Jaymie remained quite hairy. It was painful and uncomfortable whenever they removed the dressing as it pulled the hair on her skin. And if she were to have two of these PICC lines, Jaymie would have to go through this horror twice as often. Thankfully, despite the doctor's prediction, Jaymie never had to have a second PICC line placed.

The doctor also forewarned us that it would not be unusual for children receiving chemotherapy for this particular disease, to have repeated admissions to the ICU due to complications. We listened carefully to all they had to say. It was difficult to process all this information. We had a lot on our plate as it was, and we did not have any energy left to worry about the future. Until that day, I had never thought that exhaustion could be a blessing from our loving God. We lived our lives one day at a time; that was all we could do. Once again, Jaymie defied the statistics. Throughout her prolonged illness and treatment, she did not spend a single minute in the ICU.

I spent a lot of time praying and meditating throughout this entire journey as I had a surplus of idle time; times when I could not do anything about everything. Physically, prayer was one of the few things I could actively engage in. The demands of caring for Jaymie, and my anxiety, insomnia and lack of appetite made me feel tired all the time. There was also my job that I had to continue to attend, lest I would not be able to pay our mounting medical bills. Juggling our time and attention between our sick child and our two others was no easy task. Through all these, I learned how to be patient, as I had to wait for almost everything, from Jaymie's test results, her response to treatment, or simply, better days.

My brokenness and helplessness made me yearn for God. Nothing else in this life gave me any relief from this seemingly endless nightmare. I found God as I searched for a way to escape my misery. Talking and listening to God allowed me to constantly feel His presence because He always engaged me in a loving conversation. Praying gave me rest. It gave me peace. It gave me strength. It gave me courage. It provided me everything I needed that I did not have.

During one of my prayers and meditations, I somehow visualized myself hanging on to a tree branch sticking out the side of a mountain. I looked down and saw a burning truck hundreds of feet below me. God asked me to let go. Out of fear, I refused, as my fate was obvious if I did. God insisted, but I continued to resist. I was petrified. He encouraged me to trust Him. There was not much of a choice left for me, as I was getting weaker and could not hang on much longer. Eventually, I completely surrendered my fate to God and let go of the branch. I immediately experienced a peace I never imagined I could. I lost the fear. My anxiety evaporated. The act of making that conscious decision to surrender gave me relief.

I still remember this vision from time to time. It reminds me of what having a "reckless faith" can do. Trusting God completely, even when it did not make sense, gave me a sense of peace almost instantly. As my relationship with God developed through the reading of scriptures and experiencing His love and faithfulness, it became easier to make sense of trusting God. I started searching relentlessly for clues about God's character in the scriptures and tried to find out how He responded to different situations. If He indeed is the same yesterday, today, and forever (Hebrews 13:8), I sure would want to know how He was yesterday to know how He would be to me today and tomorrow. Eventually, seeking God's guidance and intervention became my first option and not my last resort anymore. I stopped letting my human limitations limit what I think God could do. Despite gaining these insights, I still struggle with having a courageous faith when I need to have it. But I do not see this as a failure. Life is my training ground to help build my endurance and increase my faith. Slowly but surely, I continue to move closer to my goal.

"But blessed is the one who trusts in the LORD, whose confidence is in him. They will be like a tree planted by the water that sends out its roots by the stream. It does not fear when heat comes; its leaves are always green. It has no worries in a year of drought and never fails to bear fruit." (Jeremiah 17:7-8 NIV)

Newton's third law, which states that for every

action there is an equal and opposite reaction, applies to our daily struggles in life. For every difficulty we faced during Jaymie's illness, there was always love, comfort, and help that came alongside the pain. The paradox of it all, was feeling most loved by God when we hurt the most. The more we hurt, the more He comforted us. The more we lacked, the more He bestowed. But could it be that God always gave abundantly, we just never paid attention until we were in dire straits?

We often took many things in life for granted and considered them as trivial. But many of these endowed us with so much joy and hope during those dark days in the hospital. Who would have thought that being able to pick food from the hospital menu could give us so much to look forward to each day? Every morning, Jaymie was given a menu from which she was able to pick what she wanted for each meal. The food they served was nothing out of the ordinary, but the fact that she was given a choice gave her a sense of control. It was one of the few things that kept her somewhat excited, despite the bleakness of her situation. And when she got tired of eating the same food or when she just did not feel like eating, Jaymie relished picking out something that my wife and I might enjoy. The loss of control during one's illness can be very discouraging and regaining it in one form or another can be quite comforting. During her multiple hospitalizations, there were many other examples when she was able to gain some control of her life. Every Wednesday, the children were given a piece of paper to write down their wish list of toys and gifts. The following day, one of their wishes would come true. Only in this hospital can one be in the midst of a nightmare and yet have a chance of living a beautiful magical dream life, at least once a week. Jaymie also had her favorite nurses, and we were very grateful for those days when the head nurse would make every effort to grant her request for a specific nurse, whenever possible. One nurse in particular, Ms. Christy Miller, provided excellent nursing care and showed genuine love and compassion to Jaymie, and Jaymie reciprocated just as much. There were also many others who made a difference in Jaymie's life during those difficult days in the hospital. They included doctors, nurses, teachers, volunteers, social workers, cafeteria workers, and janitors. All of them gave what they had a lot of -- pure love. By their doing so, we felt God's presence and we saw the many faces of God. It is ironic that God's face can be so clear when our days were so dark.

There were many more people who supported and walked with us through this journey. Family, friends, co-workers, and acquaintances visited or called us. They brought us food, gave Jaymie gifts to cheer her up, and kept her entertained through her lengthy hospital stay. They kept us company and encouraged us. One of our neighbors took our trash bin back to our house every Monday after collection. He did it anonymously, and I only found out who it was after I had time to review our security camera recordings several weeks later. Another of our neighbors volunteered to pick up our other two kids in the morning and took them to school. Several people donated whole blood and platelet or helped organize blood drives for direct donations to Jaymie. Because Jaymie had received hundreds of pints of blood and platelet throughout her illness, she had developed antibodies and could not accept certain subtypes of blood. Furthermore, there was always a shortage of blood products. Blood is always a valuable commodity, especially to those like Jaymie, who could not make their own. Blood truly is life. No blood, no life. Jaymie's bone marrow had shut down entirely and she needed outside sources of blood to live. I will never forget those people who sacrificed their comfort and convenience to donate blood for her, and those who helped make it happen. Donating platelet is particularly difficult. The process takes several hours and can really drain the donor's energy. My taekwondo mentor and friend, Chief Master Ken Reynolds, volunteered numerous times to help Jaymie out especially during those times when she needed it most. He told me that he would always be available and ready to donate blood for Jaymie even at a short moment's notice. These people who donated blood for Jaymie, truly shared their life with her. The love and help we received from all these people were constant reminders of God's love and faithfulness. He kept His promise that He would always be there to protect us, lift us up, and give us rest when we need it. God moved these people's hearts to move ours.

"Even though I walk through the darkest valley, I will fear no evil, for you are with me; your rod and your staff, they comfort me." Psalm 23:4 NIV.

As the chemotherapy progressed, Jaymie started losing her hair, as expected. What was not expected though was, for several weeks, only the hair on the back part of her head fell off. When she looked at the mirror, she still looked relatively the same. This gave her time to adjust and accept the adverse physical effects of the chemotherapy. The only time she was reminded of her hair loss was when she saw the clumps of hair on her pillow. We tried to clean them up as soon as we saw them so as not to distress her. Over time, she started to lose hair in front as well, and there was no way to hide it from her. There was one saving grace though. She had a few long strands of hair in front that never fell off. This allowed her to flip it aside or run her fingers through it, as if she still had a full head of hair. This residual hair comforted her throughout her treatment and illness. We left those few strands of hair the way they were throughout her illness to comfort Jaymie and to remind us of God's love and mercy.

Yes, the suffering continued, but God's blessings also continued to pour down upon us. Those were very painful days of our lives that we would never want to relive, and yet, somehow, in some ways, we did not necessarily want to forget them, either. In a crazy sense, we were in pain but happy, even though we were not happy to be in pain. And as we walked on shattered glasses during those dark and seemingly endless days and nights, we stuck to the daily pledge we made as a family. "We will obey God's will. We will trust God's wisdom. We will thank, praise, and worship God always."

CHAPTER 11
WHEN FAITH CAN'T BE FOUND

It was tough to watch our precious baby girl suffer needlessly. We could not understand why it had to be us. What had we done to deserve so much sorrow and suffering? We felt helpless. We could not ease Jaymie's pain. The future was uncertain. Was she going to get better? Was she even going to live? God had the power to fix this mess, but would He? God could hear our cries, but why was He so silent? How could He bear to watch us suffer?

Like many parents of sick children or anyone going through difficult times, we questioned God's purpose. My wife felt betrayed by God and was very angry. I felt that God was pruning me, disciplining me, and sometimes, I wondered if He was punishing me.

We lived in the hospital for months at a time.

Caring for Jaymie's daily needs and dealing with the uncertainties of her future overwhelmed us. I spent all my remaining energy praying, while my wife, Josephine, spent hers reading about Jaymie's illness and searching for answers in medical literature. This eventually escalated to the point of her resenting me for engaging in what she thought was the useless exercise of prayer, which in her mind, equated to giving up or doing nothing.

One day, she typed in one of the websites she visited frequently to search for answers and new treatments. To her surprise, instead of seeing a list of medical journal entries, a video started playing. A tour guide in Israel was showing the place where Abraham brought Isaac to be sacrificed as a burnt offering to God. He talked about Abraham's total obedience to God's will and God's promise to bless him with descendants as numerous as the stars. My wife was shocked and could not understand how this video surfaced like this out of nowhere. It was strange, and yet that was what she needed at that time. She called out for me to look at the computer screen and help her make sense of it. She was sure that she typed in the correct web address as she had done so many times before. I reckoned that she might have accidentally hit the wrong key and navigated to a different website. However, the link to the video on the webpage, positioned in an obscure area, was not easy to find. Furthermore, after clicking the link, there was a relatively long introduction before getting to the part of the video that my wife viewed. We could not come up with a logical explanation.

I guess we really did not need an explanation. My wife came to believe and accept that God must have intervened here as an act of grace and love for her. She broke down and cried, and later told me that for the first time in a long while, she felt the loving presence of God. For the first time since Jaymie's illness, she was willing to give God a chance to prove Himself that He truly loved us and cared about us.

Chapter 12
When a Touch Became God's

Jaymie had recurring high fevers throughout her illness. Each time, we rushed her to the hospital where she underwent a battery of tests to check for possible infections and treated with intravenous antibiotics. Her white blood cell count (WBC), the type of blood cell that fights infections, was very low due to her bone marrow failure caused by the disease. This made her susceptible to infections spreading to her bloodstream and compromising the function of her organs.

One time, the doctors felt it was safe for Jaymie to go home as she was doing relatively well. They thought it would be good for her mentally to get a break from being in the hospital and be back to familiar surroundings. It was also a relief for us to sleep in our own beds. It can be very distressing to be confined to a hospital room for months. It is depressing enough to be sick, but adding the social isolation, the level of desperation is exacerbated ten-fold. We savored every minute of our time at home, no matter how short.

One morning, before I left for work, I checked on Jaymie and kissed her goodbye. To my dismay, she felt hot and did not look well. I suspected that she had a high fever. I knew we would have to take her back to the emergency room. I alerted my wife and asked her to get ready. We went through this kind of crisis so often that we always had an overnight bag with all the things we needed packed. In most cases, Jaymie ended up having to be admitted and stay in the hospital for an extended period of time.

In the meantime, I sat by Jaymie and comforted her. I laid my hands on her head and prayed over her. The sense of impending doom and panic paralyzed me. All I could say was "In Jesus' most powerful name, please help Jaymie's temperature to come down." I must have repeated this line a million times, it seemed. I shut my eyes tight, and I desperately cried out for God to intervene. When I finally opened my eyes, with my hand still on Jaymie's head, I saw steam rising between my fingers. It was unreal. My mind went blank and felt dull, and then I experienced a sense of calm and peace. Suddenly, I realized that Jaymie's forehead felt cooler, and her color returned. I stood slowly and went downstairs to tell my wife to check Jaymie's temperature. I told her we may not need to go to the hospital anymore. She wondered what was going on. All I could say to her at that time was Jaymie's fever broke. I did not know how to explain what had happened. I was still trying to wrap my head around all that had just transpired. My wife brought a thermometer and checked Jaymie's temperature. It was normal.

impaired because of her very low WBC. Despite strong intravenous antibiotics, the extent and reach of the infection deepened and widened. There was always concern about the infection traveling into her bloodstream, causing sepsis. Another major concern was the infection deepening to form a tract that connects with the large intestines called a fistula. My wife diligently cleaned the area with antiseptic and applied antibiotic ointment multiple times a day. It was a heroic task, and I was thankful that she was so dedicated and determined to do what she could to help Jaymie heal from the infection. It certainly helped that she is a pediatrician and knew what to do.

Despite everyone's best efforts, Jaymie's perianal abscess continued to get worse. The doctor wanted to do a CT scan to assess the extent of the infection and determine whether surgery was necessary. This was not what we wanted to hear. Jaymie would surely object to having a CT scan. She knew quite well whenever she had one of these procedures done, we would be asked to leave the room, and she would have to deal with the doctors and nurses by herself. We already knew how Jaymie would react once she found out about the plans we had agreed to on her behalf. We knew she would not be happy, and her reaction would not be pretty. Furthermore, the thought of possibly needing surgery concerned us gravely. With her low platelet count, she could bleed easily from any surgical procedure. Infection and delayed wound healing were serious concerns as well because of her low WBC. It was overwhelming for us as parents just thinking of all these potential obstacles on the horizon.

So, the date and time of the CT scan was set. I rearranged my work schedule to allow me to be there to support Jaymie and to assist my wife. I also arranged provisions to care for our other two kids, and made sure they were picked up from school, fed, and entrusted to relatives or friends.

On the day of the CT scan, everything in the hours leading to the test went as well as possible. Jaymie was calm and in good spirits. My wife managed her anxieties well. I secretly panicked, but somehow, I held everything together. We spared our other two kids the stress we were experiencing by only giving them information that was pertinent.

As usual, my sister-in-law, Jennifer, and brother-in-law, Patrick, saved the day. They agreed to watch over Tyler and Julienne for as long as we needed. The kids were excited to be with their cousins and enjoyed the spoiling by their aunt and uncle. I dropped the kids off and quickly returned to the hospital.

Reality set in as I found myself alone in the silence inside my car. My thoughts raced, and they were mostly negative. An endless number of "what-ifs" filled my mind as I went through the possible outcomes of the test. I vacillated from feelings of despair to hope. One moment, I was resigned to accepting a no-win fate; the next, I believed a miracle was possible and developing.

I drove down the highway, focusing intently on the road ahead but distracted by fear-filled thoughts. Out of nowhere, an orange-brown butterfly flew across my line of vision, made a sharp ninety degree turn to face me, and flew straight at me hitting the windshield of the car. I could almost swear I stared into its face. It sure may sound ridiculous, but it seemed like our eyes locked for a second before it went charging toward me, hitting the windshield.

I did not think much of what had just happened. It was strange, but I had more important things to be concerned about at the time. I continued driving, as I was in a hurry to be at the hospital in time for Jaymie's CT scan appointment. As I took the first exit off the highway, the same exact occurrence I just described above, happened again. This time, I could not ignore the strangeness of it. I quickly called my wife to tell her what had just happened. It was so unusual, I had to tell someone. I felt like I lost my mind. As I was sharing the details with her, yet another identical butterfly struck my windshield for the third time in the same exact way. I must have sounded startled and confused on the phone. After I had time to settle down, I suddenly felt a tremendous amount of peace. It was as if the butterflies were sent by God to comfort me, and I was convinced that everything was going to be okay.

At the hospital, Jaymie was wheeled into the CT scan room. She was animated by the artwork in the room and instantly noticed the butterflies painted on the walls. This comforted her as my recent butterfly experience did me. Jaymie was very cooperative during the CT scan. Up to this point, everything went smoothly, beyond our expectations. However, the results were not as we had hoped, as the scan showed that she had already developed a fistula, and this would require surgery to place a drain created using parts from a cadaver. We arranged an appointment with a surgeon, a decision we did not want to have to make, but there were no alternatives. This was needed to avoid further complications.

We were discouraged, anxious, and nervous. We barely ate nor slept. Jaymie's tedious wound care routine was probably the only thing that gave us a sense of control and predictability. However, that predictability went out the window during the early morning hours the day of her surgery.

Jaymie got up to urinate at around 2 a.m. My wife followed her to the bathroom so she could clean up the wound afterwards like she always did. As she carried out her usual routine, my wife noticed a big, white, fleshy "thing" hanging off Jaymie's right buttock where the wound was. It looked like a chunk of string cheese. She tugged at it, causing it to elongate as she pulled. My wife became nervous and yelled for me to help. She thought she tore something up when she pulled it. I rushed to her side to check what was happening. The big chunk of tissue I saw looked very unusual, but it did not appear like torn up flesh. We both decided it was likely safe to continue to pull it out as long as there was no resistance and Jaymie did not hurt. And so, we did. We pulled out all we could until there was nothing left to pull. We both stared at this "thing" in front of us. There was no blood. It did not smell. It was just a big white chunk of something. Jaymie's right buttock where this "thing" came out from flattened.

Later that morning, we went to see the surgeon for the procedure and explained what had happened a few hours earlier. The doctor examined Jaymie's buttock and decided to cancel the planned surgery. A follow-up CT scan was later done, and this showed that the abscess around the rectum and anus was no longer present. The fistula had collapsed, and it was thought that this would likely heal up on its own eventually.

Much of what we dreaded did not come to pass. Jaymie did not throw a tantrum when we told her she would have to have another CT scan. She was actually calm and cheerful in the CT scan room, thanks to the butterfly paintings on the wall. Most importantly, she did not require surgery anymore. God answered our prayers in a manner that we could not have designed even if He had given us absolute freedom to choose the outcome. We prayed for healing the way we imagined how it could happen. That is, the surgery would be done safely without complications, and it will effectively and eventually heal the fistula with the help of continued antibiotic treatment. Instead, Jaymie was granted instant healing, without surgery, through an early morning scare that led her two frightened parents digging out her perianal abscess with their bare hands.

This experience taught us to never again underestimate what God can do because we let the limitations of our minds dictate our expectations. Through this, God reminded us that even though He may allow difficulties in our lives for whatever purpose He may have, He will provide us with the peace and comfort we need to make it through.

CHAPTER 14
THE BUTTERFLY PROPHECY

At the beginning of Jaymie's illness, I asked God for a sign to let me know that all would be well. I know this sounds weak and exposed my lack of faith, but in a dire situation like ours, it was easy to crumble under the weight. Nevertheless, God did answer and sent butterflies, presenting them in the most unusual circumstances. Despite this, I continued to doubt. Were the butterflies truly God's response to my request for reassurance? All this would definitely not pass scientific scrutiny. It would take faith to believe that this was God's declaration of His promise. My problem was, I did not have enough faith. My whole being was consumed with fear and anxiety. Hence, I continued to plead with God to give me an undeniable sign and maybe some kind of direct reassurance that Jaymie would be completely healed.

A few months later, during one of my deep conversations with God, He told me that He would specifically send a butterfly to the window of Jaymie's hospital room on the fourth floor of the building. This would be His affirmation that the first sign was from Him. Maybe this was all wishful thinking, and my compromised mind made this all up. Nevertheless, I truly believed that this message came from God, and I was sure that I would see that butterfly on the window before we left the hospital, and I told my wife accordingly. Somehow, I felt that by telling her, I was holding God to account. If He did not come through with His promise, it would be His credibility at stake.

For about five and a half weeks, Jaymie had a large abscess on her left eyelid. She did not have adequate white blood cells to fight off even the simplest infections. Strong intravenous antibiotics were pumped into her blood to keep the infection at bay. She was tired of being in the hospital for months on end. At one point, it looked like she was responding to the treatment, and the doctor was getting her ready for discharge. We started packing our belongings and the toys she accumulated during her extended hospitalization. As the day of our departure came closer, Jaymie was in great spirits. She was excited at the prospect of finally being able to return home and sleep in her own bed. She was sick of hospital food, blood draws, early morning vital signs checks, and the never-ending other tests that she had to endure. Finally, she would get a respite from all these situations. My wife and I also wanted so badly to return home. On the day of her discharge, with all of us dressed up and ready to go, the nurse arrived to check Jaymie's temperature. Lo and behold, she spiked a fever again; we were devastated. Jaymie started bawling and was inconsolable. It was good that Tyler, Julienne, and her grandma were there to console her. My wife was eventually able to calm her down and took her on a stroller ride around the hospital ward. In the meantime, she asked me to go buy Jaymie's favorite pepperoni pizza at the mall.

While I was at the mall, my cellphone rang. I answered, and Tyler was shouting on the other end of the line asking me to hurry back to the hospital. I went into panic mode. What now? What new emergency has come up? I tried to calm Tyler down so he could tell me exactly what was happening. In the meantime, I hurried as fast as I could back to the hospital. Tyler managed to explain that "Mommy said your butterfly is at the window!" I asked him to stay on the phone with me and describe what he was looking at. Even though I knew it did not make sense, I asked him to tell everyone to stay still so the butterfly would not fly away before I got back there. At least I had the presence of mind to ask him to take as many pictures as he could. When I reached the elevator, Tyler told me that the butterfly had just flown away. I suddenly lost my adrenaline rush. When the elevator opened, and I made it back to where my family was gathered, I found them staring out the window. The kids, including Jaymie, were very excited to have seen the butterfly. This happened on the fourth floor as God had told me it would be. My wife was speechless and in tears. We both knew the significance of this. Although I was disappointed that I did not get to see the butterfly, I knew that God meant this for my wife and children.

As we were going through our own trials and tribulations, I discovered that one of my friends' son was also fighting for his life in a hospital in Alabama. He had contracted E. coli O157:H7 infection and had gone into kidney failure. One night, as I was driving back to the hospital after dropping off our other two children home, I suddenly felt the need to call my friend, Rob, to get an update on his son's situation. It was 10:30 at night and I felt awkward about calling him so late. However, I felt this extreme restlessness pushing me to call him regardless, so I did. Rob answered, and I shared with him our butterfly story and how God touched our hearts. It gave me a sense of purpose to use our pain to encourage a friend and give him strength to deal with his own battle.

A few days later, I got an unexpected mid-morning call from Rob. He sounded really excited. He is a gastroenterologist like me; in fact, he was my former student. Rob was in his endoscopy suite performing a colonoscopy when he happened to briefly glance to one side of the room and saw a big, blue butterfly on the window. He immediately knew what this meant based on our recent conversation. He was deeply moved. Like

CHAPTER 15

COLORFUL REMINDERS
OF GOD'S PROMISE

Over the next several months, we were inundated with butterflies everywhere we went. We started to wonder where they originated; we had never seen so many in our lives. Even our family and close friends who had ministered to us were visited by these beautiful angels. And yes, even the skeptics among us got to experience the butterflies.

As I drove to work each day, I was frequently greeted by butterflies along the way. They were either flying around me, or sometimes, flying at a low altitude right in front of my car. When this happened, I had to slow down or steer away from them. I recalled one time, there was even a swarm of them that flew by me. I had never seen anything like this in my life.

Once, I commented to my wife about these sightings. She told me that these were normal occurrences, and that I was putting too much meaning behind them. She may be correct. All these months of stress may have altered my perception of things. Notwithstanding, I felt misunderstood and deeply disappointed. I had hoped that she would share my excitement and see God's hands at work. Because of this, I drove to the chapel to soothe my hurt feelings by spending some quiet time in prayer. As I exited the chapel, I was greeted by a beautiful pair of butterflies dancing together. They flew in unison as if they were holding each other's "hands." That made me smile.

One of my nieces dreamt about Jaymie while she was very sick. She woke up feeling sad for her. As she went outside their house, a yellow butterfly came directly to her. She knew that her mom, my wife's sister, would want to hear about this and so she recounted the event. One day, her mom shared this and our other butterfly stories with one of her co-workers, who was very cynical about it. I could not really blame her. As soon as she was done expressing her skepticism, she noticed something on top of my sister-in-law's handbag. They both looked at it and were stunned to see a beautiful butterfly calmly resting on the leather.

A childhood friend of mine who was not spiritually inclined was also skeptical about topics like this. His wife, however, was moved by our faith journey and enjoyed listening to the fun butterfly stories I shared. One day, someone rang their doorbell, which she answered. When she opened the door, there was a white butterfly on the door. She then went to her garden to tend to the flowerbed and noticed a group of white butterflies following her. Later that day, she told her husband what happened as she felt those sightings were unusual. He told her that she had become too engrossed with our butterfly stories, and it was affecting her interpretation of everyday events. Then, something caught his attention that made him pause. There was a butterfly on the window right beside them. He later admitted that this random event suddenly meant something to him. He went from being a skeptic to believing that God must be using these seemingly ordinary occurrences in unusual circumstances to inspire him to grow in his faith.

At the Arkansas Children's Hospital, a day was set aside for patients and their siblings to select whichever toys they liked. Our kids were generally timid, and they did not pick any. Surprisingly, later in the afternoon, someone knocked on the door and said, "I thought you might like these." He presented us with two battery-operated bottles, each containing a fake, flying monarch butterfly. We did not know this person, and he certainly did not know the significance of butterflies to us.

I had a patient who came to see me in the office during the time when Jaymie was very ill. She did not know anything about our special encounters with butterflies. That particular day, she wore earrings and bracelets decorated with pink butterflies. Out of curiosity, I asked her what made her wear all those accessories. She told me that as she was getting ready to come and see me, she felt God had nudged her to wear them that day.

On two occasions, I had a "butterfly encounter" while I was sharing my testimony about God's love and faithfulness to us during Jaymie's illness. The first, while I was parked outside a church. A friend of mine invited me to attend their church service on a Monday night. While talking inside the car, a yellow butterfly appeared from nowhere, and hit my windshield. The second was a time when one of our employees from the business department visited my office to check on me and see how our daughter was doing. While we were talking, a large, brown butterfly suddenly hit my office window. Both of us were startled by this. As soon as we realized what had happened, we thanked God for the constant reminder of His love and the comfort He provides.

Jaymie loved her butterflies. They made her happy. They were like her guardian angels. When she was scared, they calmed her down. When she was frustrated, they gave her hope. One day, as she was walking towards her homeschool teacher's front door to drop off her homework, a large monarch butterfly landed on her bald head and stayed there for an extended period. It was surreal. Jaymie was so animated by it. It made her so happy. It must have been like being touched by God.

There are basically two types of people in this world; those who believe every unusual experience is a miracle, and those who see these occurrences as just that, random unrelated moments of chance. I see God's fingerprints all over these hard-to-explain occurrences. I believe that God sent them to comfort us by making us feel His presence, to remind us of His promises and His faithfulness, and to inspire us to believe in His goodness and power. These butterfly stories helped us because in them we felt the overwhelming love of God. They made us happy, and they gave us hope when we desperately needed it.

CHAPTER 16
THE CURE FOR PTSD

We could not figure out why Jaymie was urinating so frequently. She could not get a good night's sleep because of this. It was hard on my wife as well. At night, she would get up to assist Jaymie every time she needed to go to the bathroom. She also had to clean her meticulously so as not to worsen the infection on her right buttock. Initially, the doctors thought she might have been getting too much intravenous (IV) fluids, hence, they lowered the infusion rate. This did not help. She was checked for urinary tract infection, but that was not it either. Soon, it became apparent. Jaymie was in acute kidney failure as indicated by the rapid rise in her kidney function test. There is a phase before the onset of kidney failure wherein the kidney cannot absorb fluids, and excessive amount of urine is excreted. That explained her unusual urinary frequency. This was devastating. First it was bone marrow failure, then liver failure, and now, kidney failure. How much more suffering can anyone take? When the chemotherapy for HLH started, we were hopeful, anticipating a positive outcome. However, it seemed that whenever things started to improve, we would be disappointed again. Each battle left it harder to be hopeful again.

We did not see this coming, but hindsight is always 20/20. In retrospect, there were clues and warnings that we had overlooked. As you will later see, even this was part of God's bigger plan.

When Jaymie had her CT scan to check for complications related to her perianal abscess, the radiologist mentioned that there was some unusual change to her kidneys. It was non-specific and he could not make a definitive diagnosis. None of us, including the doctors, had thought of the possibility that Jaymie was experiencing an ongoing kidney injury.

At the time, she was getting some powerful antibiotics for an extended period to treat her perianal abscess, some of which have serious potential side effects. One, in particular, required her to be closely monitored and its dose adjusted accordingly. At one point, Jaymie was well enough to be discharged from the hospital, and we continued administering the antibiotics at home. An infusion company delivered the medicine to us weekly. Every time they handed us the week's supply, they would always ask us if Jaymie had her "blood tests" done. She got blood tests so often that we naturally answered "yes."

The night she was re-admitted to the hospital due to acute kidney failure, a nurse was going over her chart and noticed that her Vancomycin level had not been checked in a while. This antibiotic is potentially toxic to the kidneys when its level exceeds a certain amount. My wife and I are both very familiar with this drug. Jaymie's treating physicians are excellent doctors who were very thorough and attentive. How could we all have missed this? The nurse quickly submitted Jaymie's blood to test her Vancomycin level, and it came back very high. It became apparent then that it was the cause of her acute kidney failure. The IV contrast they injected during the CT scan could have also aggravated the injury to the kidneys. Through all of this, if we only had enough faith in God, we would have been able to see that He has a grand plan for us. But we were physically and mentally exhausted. We had no strength left in us to draw from. We could not intellectualize all this suffering. There seemed to be no end in sight, and we were losing hope. This vicious cycle of misfortune gave me pangs of anxiety and sometimes, panic attacks.

A kidney specialist was called in to evaluate Jaymie. He reviewed her history and test results and candidly told us that it would take at least six weeks for her kidneys to recover. There was no medicine to assist. She was given IV fluids to flush her kidneys, the offending agent was discontinued, and other medications that might be toxic to the kidneys were avoided. We had to patiently wait and pray that with time her kidneys would heal themselves. In one week, her kidney function miraculously normalized, and she was discharged from the hospital. We were ecstatic and once again, hopeful. But at the back of our minds, we wondered how long would this last?

Jaymie had her follow-up blood test done one week later at the outpatient clinic. I had to return to work and so my wife went with her. They waited nervously for the results. The doctor entered the room and broke the bad news. She was in kidney failure again and had to be re-admitted to the hospital. Jaymie became very upset as she could not stand being back in the hospital. My wife needed some support. She was very discouraged and anxious. She called me and asked me to come and be with them as they waited for a hospital bed to become available. I left my office in a hurry to meet up with them. I was tired of this old routine. We get some relief, and then crisis hits again. We barely had time to enjoy some good news only to be met with further disappointment. Just when we were starting to feel hopeful, our hopes get crushed without warning. My wife and I would wake up every morning with our hearts trying to burst out of our chests. It was a very uncomfortable feeling. It was like we had post-traumatic stress disorder (PTSD). We were desperately looking for peace in our lives. If this had to go on for much longer, we pleaded with God to give us a little break to regain our strength. We needed time to recharge and regroup before we could face another battle.

When I arrived at the hospital, I ran as quickly as I could through the maze to get to the clinic where Jaymie and my wife were. There were many people in the lobby and hallways, and the crowd slowed me down. My heart was pounding, and I was sweating profusely. My mind felt numb, and my ears were buzzing. Suddenly, out of nowhere, I heard this loud, thunderous voice saying, "Did I not tell you that I am trying to cure your PTSD?" The voice was so loud that I literally stopped in my tracks. I was shocked and confused at first, but after I had settled down, I wondered if this was the voice of God. Maybe I was hallucinating, but the words were so clear. Perhaps the extreme stress of the moment led to this surreal experience. I scoured the internet for discussions on this topic, and I was surprised to find that in one report, one in ten people interviewed reported having heard God's audible voice. The voice I heard must have been God's. It gave me so much peace and comfort. I somehow came to believe again that everything would be okay.

Once a hospital bed became available, Jaymie was transported to her room. We knew all the staff in the Hematology and Oncology ward very well. For about eight months, the hospital was our home away from home. Even though they were sad that Jaymie was sick again, they were also happy to see us. The kidney specialist went to check on Jaymie; he was cautious about his assessment and told us that it was just going to take more time. There was nothing we could do but wait. Tincture of time was the only treatment available. We decided we would take it day by day, and we would keep praying, believing, and hoping. Hope was the only thing that made each day bearable.

In about three days, Jaymie's kidney function test normalized, and it stayed that way.

For several months, we were trapped in this vicious cycle of pain, brief relief, and recurrence of pain. We started to doubt whether we would ever experience lasting relief from our sufferings. We began to believe that good news is a premonition for bad news to come. So, how did God cure our PTSD? He allowed us to go through the same dilemma, but this time, He surprised us with a different and unexpected positive outcome. He gave us a new experience upon which to base our hope on, from this point forward. The seed of faith started to germinate, and the plant of peace began to emerge and break through the soil. Because of this, I know for sure that the thunderous voice I heard, was the audible voice of God.

CHAPTER 17
NINTH DOSE OF CHEMOTHERAPY

Hemophagocytic lymphohistiocytosis (HLH) is a rare disease causing the immune system to attack multiple organs of the body including the liver, brain, and bone marrow. In 2012, the treatment protocol required eight weeks of a potent and toxic chemotherapeutic agent. For those who have the inherited or familial type of the disease, treatment continues until a bone marrow transplantation is done.

During the course of Jaymie's treatment, her doctor submitted blood samples to Cincinnati Children's Hospital to test for the five genes associated with the familial type of HLH. This would determine if she would need continued chemotherapy beyond the eight weeks prescribed under the protocol. Cincinnati Children's was the only center that could run these tests at the time. Because of this and the complexity of the tests, the results were expected to take a while before they become available. Despite submitting the blood samples early on, after six weeks of treatment, we were still without results. We were beginning to get anxious. The familial type has the worst prognosis. Not only would Jaymie have to endure more of the of toxic chemotherapy, but there was also uncertainty as to whether she would need a bone marrow transplant. Neither of her siblings were a match, parents are not ideal donors, and unrelated donors are very problematic. If we were lucky and all her genetic tests were negative, the eighth dose of chemotherapy would be her last. Hence, there was an urgency for us to know this as soon as possible to spare her from having to receive further unnecessary treatment. Not knowing when the results would be available and imagining all these scenarios made it very stressful.

On her eighth week of treatment, we received news that four out of five genetic tests came back negative. At that point, the doctor only had a few more days left before he had to decide whether to infuse the ninth dose of the chemotherapy agent. He did not want to risk a relapse of the disease, hence, he recommended to proceed with infusing another dose of the chemotherapy as scheduled, if the last genetic test result did not return by then. The doctor's staff continued to make follow-up phone calls to Cincinnati Children's Hospital to obtain the result. We tried to wait very patiently, which was not easy. Every minute seemed an eternity. We could not successfully keep ourselves distracted, as the flow of negative emotions was too overwhelming.

In the meantime, I told family and friends that God was in control, and He would certainly take care of Jaymie. I dared to believe that God would not allow that ninth dose of chemotherapy to be infused. And until the first drop went into Jaymie's vein, I firmly believed that God would not allow it. I left no room for doubt and no room for God to do otherwise. I made sure every family member and friend I discussed this with knew this was how things would be. I told everyone if faith can move mountains, my faith could move two. I was confident that God would not let me down. I knew that God would do as I said He would.

Finally, the day the next dose of chemotherapy was due, we were told the machine for running the final genetic test was actually broken, preventing our receipt of the result. And so, the first drop of the chemotherapy agent entered Jaymie's vein. My heart sank, and I lost my faith in God. I was embarrassed to face my family and friends because the God I bragged about let me down and did not deliver. I was certain they would all be laughing at me because of my fanatical faith. I felt like God did this on purpose and let me fall on my face. How could He have done this to me? Did he not say that all I needed was to have faith the size of a mustard seed, and I can ask this mountain to move, and it will? I guess I was too naïve.

I was devastated, depressed, and in despair. I had no one to turn to; even God had abandoned me. As I drove down our driveway, our next-door neighbor came up to me and chatted with me while I sat helplessly in my car looking downtrodden. She tried to encourage me by reminding me how Abraham obeyed God and offered Isaac as a living sacrifice to God; how God was just testing his willingness to obey and, in the end, really did not mean to take Isaac's life. A few minutes later, Father Ralph Jones, the healing priest from Texas, called trying to comfort me and discussed the same story. This was more than just a mere coincidence; it was clear to me that God was relaying a message: maybe I was better off obeying God than making Him obey me.

I asked God to heal our child and yet I tried to stop Him from giving Jaymie another dose of chemotherapy. What if that was the answer to my prayer, that Jaymie should get nine doses of chemotherapy, instead of eight, in order to heal her completely? If that was the case, I almost derailed things. Maybe God was telling me to just trust Him and to let Him be God, and I should just be still and let Him do what He needed. My brash and reckless declaration about my faith to my loved ones was really my attempt to force God into a corner and pressure Him into doing my bidding. Thank God, He saved me from myself by not listening to me. What do we as humans know? Why do we limit God's ability to help us by asking Him to do things our way based on our limited human wisdom? It makes no sense.

A few days after the ninth infusion, the result of the last genetic test came back negative. Jaymie did not have the familial type of HLH, but she received one dose more than what the protocol required.

Chapter 18
When Only God Can Heal

One of the most difficult things I must tell a patient is, "There is nothing else I can do to help you." I had to say this to a thirty-six-year-old woman who had severe difficulty swallowing and could barely sustain herself by drinking liquids. She lost significant weight and needed something done quickly, lest she succumb to malnutrition.

I walked into the examination room to discuss the results of her tests. It was not common for a young patient like her to have such a severe problem. There were many possibilities to investigate, and I ran a battery of tests to rule them out. This was her follow-up appointment after a few weeks of testing to discuss my assessment and available treatment options. As I prepared for our meeting, I was unsure how to approach her. Giving out test results to patients is not as easy as just laying out the facts. How things are said is often more important than what is said. In the most dire situation, this could either give patients hope or leave them in total despair. Hope helps people heal and can lighten even the most unbearable conditions. Unfortunately, in this case, I had very little hope to offer. Not only was the abnormality of her swallowing very severe, there was also no obvious cause I could identify. Other than placing a feeding tube in her stomach to provide access for nutrition, there was really no treatment to correct her swallowing problem. The patient was disheartened but not necessarily surprised by the news I delivered.

Out of curiosity, I asked her how she ended up seeing me as a patient in the first place. She indicated when her health continued to decline, her primary care physician suggested she visit the Mayo Clinic for a second opinion. The patient insisted that she wanted to see me first before taking the trip to Minnesota. She told her physician that I cured her mother-in-law and believed that I could help her as well. Somehow, when she said that, I was perturbed and told her that "I have never in my life claimed to have cured anyone! Only God can." At this, the patient started to cry. I suddenly felt badly at the thought I might have offended her. The patient quickly reassured me that I did not; she was moved by what I said, and my statement confirmed her belief that God had led her to me. She was relieved that she made the right decision to see me.

The patient shared with me how difficult it was for her to schedule an appointment. Her physician requested for one on her behalf, but our office gave her a date three months in the future. She told her physician there was no way she could wait that long. The patient asked for prayers from her church that she be scheduled for a sooner appointment. They convened that night to pray with this intention. The next day, my nurse apparently called her and scheduled an appointment for the following day. They all praised God for the immediate answer to their prayers. I did recall my nurse wanting me to review her records and insist that I add her to my already packed schedule. I initially resisted because I was exhausted physically and mentally from caring for Jaymie. Out of exasperation, I acquiesced and told her to schedule the patient an appointment whenever deemed reasonable. Little did I know it was the following day. I felt embarrassed it took an entire church's prayers for me to expedite the appointment. I felt unworthy. I told the patient if she had called and asked to speak to me directly, I might have been able to spare them the inconvenience.

In the patient's best interest, I encouraged her to go to Mayo Clinic as her doctor had initially suggested. There was nothing else I could offer. Although I doubted anything more could be done, it was worth a try. They do significant research and experimental treatments. Who knows? They might be able to figure out the underlying cause or offer some form of treatment. After I made this final recommendation, I approached the door. With one foot already out the door, I suddenly remembered the anointing I received to heal the sick (I discussed this in chapter two of this book). I stood there motionless for a few seconds and debated in my mind if I should even mention it. I felt that I owed it to this lady to at least try, so I awkwardly returned to my seat.

I told the patient about Jaymie's illness and how God helped us through our darkest moments. I also shared how Father Ralph, a priest whom I had never met, anointed my hand to heal. It felt uncomfortable for a medical doctor, like me, to talk to a patient about supernatural healing. In the back of my mind, I also feared being misunderstood, something I did not need. Eventually, I found the courage to ask the patient for permission to pray over her. My voice was shaking, and I am sure my hands were, as well. On the other hand, the patient was encouraged and excited. She became hopeful. Not only did she give me permission to do this, but she was also very thankful that I dared share my faith with her.

I always carried in my pocket a vial of the healing oil that Father Ralph gave me. I anointed Jaymie's forehead with this every day. I had never prayed out loud before and I was very uncomfortable about what I was about to do. Furthermore, this anointing thing was not something that I really understood. I did not receive any training and I had not done anything like this in my life. My instinct was to say, "I could not do it," but I genuinely felt badly for this young lady who desperately needed help and was looking for hope. I felt I had to do it.

And so, I used my left thumb and made the sign of the cross with the oil on the back of my right hand and did the same on the patient's forehead with my right thumb. This was how I recalled Father Ralph instructed me. I then placed my right hand on the patient's right shoulder and prayed out loud this most embarrassing and amateur prayer. "Dear Lord, you anointed my hand to heal the sick. I don't know what to say, and I don't know what to do. This is between you and her, and I trust that you will help her get better. Amen."

At that very moment, my cellphone rang; it was my wife. She sounded excited and told me that I would not believe what had just happened. She said she had sent me a video and that I should watch it as soon as I could. I told her I was with a patient and would watch it later.

In the meantime, given that I was skeptical about this laying of hands and praying over someone for healing, I told the patient that I would go ahead and set her up for an endoscopic procedure to inject Botox into her esophagus as a last resort. Even if ineffective, it would not harm. I told her that if for some reason she felt completely fine, she could just call and cancel the procedure.

After the patient left, I viewed the video my wife sent me. It was Jaymie descending the stairs on her own and scouring the refrigerator for food. She started eating everything in sight. At the time, Jaymie was very weak and laid in bed all day. She was getting very high doses of steroids, immunosuppressive medications, and chemotherapy. Her legs were but skin and bone. Her abdomen was distended and her whole body was hairy. Her eyebrows were very thick, her cheeks were puffed up, and she only had a few strands of hair on her head. She had no strength to walk up or down the stairs on her own. Her appetite was poor, so she barely ate. Given that she had been confined to the hospital for so long, the doctor gave her permission to stay home for a few days to help her cope psychologically and maintain sanity. It helped my wife and I tremendously as well. Jaymie's sudden surge of strength, energy, and appetite, as recorded on the video was indeed a miracle. Given her grim condition, there was no way this could have happened. The most surreal aspect was that she walked down the stairs, on her own, without any help, at exactly the same time I laid my hand on my patient to pray for her healing. It was as if God's healing touch through my hand to my patient, penetrated through space and injected life into Jaymie.

A few weeks later, the patient showed up for her endoscopy appointment. I thought to myself, she must still have problems swallowing, otherwise she would not have been there. I thought to myself, "Well, at least

I prayed for her and gave her hope." As I approached the patient to prepare for the procedure, I asked her how she was doing. The patient said, "I am healed!" I asked her, "What do you mean? What happened?"

The patient told me when she left my office after I prayed over her, she knew something special had happened. The next morning, she was able to drink her protein shake for breakfast and was ecstatic that she did not regurgitate it as usual. The patient was convinced she had truly been cured. In her excitement, she told her husband she would be going to their nearby Subway to get a turkey sandwich. For the first time in years, she enjoyed eating solid food. She called all her church friends and shared the unbelievable blessing God had bestowed her. They all praised God together for the miraculous healing.

The patient told me that she decided to come for her endoscopy appointment because she wanted to share her story with me in person. When I evaluated her, she still had a residual ache in her upper abdomen, even though she could swallow normally. I told her since she was already there, we should inject the Botox into her lower esophagus as originally planned. Besides, I was still a bit skeptical whether she was truly healed by prayer alone. It would have been quackery for me to chart that I had cancelled the planned procedure because she was supernaturally healed through prayer.

Two months later, the patient returned to my office for her follow-up visit. She was still able to swallow normally, but the knot-like sensation on her upper abdomen persisted. At that point, I insisted that she pursue making an appointment at Mayo Clinic. Honestly, I just wanted to feel better knowing that someone else evaluated her objectively and confirmed that everything that could be done was indeed done. I do believe prayers are powerful and miracles do happen, but I was also sure God would have wanted me to do my due diligence in aiding the patient.

So, the patient went to Mayo Clinic and underwent two weeks of extensive evaluation. They repeated many of the tests, including the swallowing study. The only significant result they found was constipation. The swallowing test they repeated showed her esophagus motility was now completely normal. On the surface, the cost of traveling, enduring the discomfort of repeated tests, and finding essentially nothing wrong may seem like wasted time and expense. But for this patient, I am sure it was well worth it to get confirmation of the miracle she had received.

Chapter 19
The Power of "Yes"

During a day I was assigned to do consultations at the hospital, I saw a patient in liver failure due to a long history of alcohol abuse. I was asked to assess whether he had any hope for a meaningful recovery from his dire illness. His abdomen was filled with large amounts of fluid that seeped from the surface of his liver. His legs were massively swollen from fluid retention, and he could barely move them. On the CT scan of his abdomen, the patient's liver was almost completely replaced by tumors. Two of three cancer markers were positive by blood test. His doctor suspected he might have a primary cancer elsewhere that metastasized to his liver. When I saw him, he was vomiting fresh blood, his vital signs were unstable, and he was in kidney failure. The patient was critically ill, and the prognosis was grave.

First on my order of priorities was to figure out quickly where the bleeding originated and try to stop it if I could. In patients with liver disease, the cause of upper gastrointestinal bleeding is often from ruptured engorged veins in the esophagus, called varices. Based on statistics, about seventy percent of patients succumb to this. As soon as I studied his condition, I decided to do an emergency endoscopy. His entire esophagus was severely ulcerated. Fortunately, it did not appear that he bled from ruptured esophageal varices. Fresh blood was squirting from somewhere in the esophagus, and the large pool of blood made it impossible for me to identify the point of bleeding for treatment. The patient was hemorrhaging, and I was almost certain I would lose him. It was sheer chaos in the room. I yelled out orders one after another as I struggled to stabilize the patient while I continued to find ways to stop the bleeding. A breathing tube was inserted into his airway to protect him from drowning in his own blood. Time was running out. As the bleeding continued, I became less optimistic, but I knew I could not give up. Then, just when I thought all hope was gone, the bleeding suddenly slowed down enough for me to identify the source and treat it.

Although he survived this acute event, the patient remained confined to the hospital due to his fluid retention issue. It was a significant challenge managing his water pills as they could potentially worsen his already compromised kidney function. He required a higher dose of the medicine than we could safely give him. While the fluid in his abdomen could be drained frequently through a catheter, the severe swelling of his legs could only be managed by increasing the dose of his water pills. Weeks went by, and the patient did not make significant progress. His abdomen was still very distended, and he was quite uncomfortable. He was unable to move around much due to the heaviness and stiffness of his swollen lower extremities. The patient was getting discouraged. It also did not help that he rarely had visitors. He became depressed and withdrawn.

Thankfully, the patient's bleeding problem did not recur. His kidney function remained poor but was stable. Two separate biopsies of the liver masses and several abdominal fluid analyses were done weeks apart and did not yield evidence of cancer. There was also no cancer found outside of the liver. The only reason he could not leave the hospital was because we could not control the fluid build-up in his abdomen and legs.

On one of those long nights making rounds in the hospital, I found myself highly irritable as I went to check on this patient. The nurses were supposed to weigh him every morning and record the information on his chart. The trend of his daily weighing helped me evaluate whether he was eliminating or retaining fluids. From this, I determined how many water pills he would require. Despite repeated orders to perform this important task, it was neglected for the third day in a row. I lost my temper and let everybody at the nurse's station know how unhappy I was. I was quite certain that none of those nurses there would say I was a nice and kind man. In the midst of my outburst, I felt God whisper to me to go to the patient's room and pray with him. At first, I ignored it. I thought I must have been imagining things as I was tired, and my blood sugar must have been low. I stayed focused on completing my work as it was getting late, and I wanted to leave the hospital so badly to grab something to eat. However, the nagging thought of being asked to pray with the patient remained and was very unnerving. It reached the point where I could not focus on my tasks. I then decided to confront God asking, "Is it really You who is asking me to pray with this patient? It's nine o'clock! I haven't had anything to eat. I want to go home. I'm tired." I also did not feel I could pray with someone following my tantrum a few minutes prior. I did not feel I could pray at all, whether alone or with anyone. It felt like God was not intimidated by my defiance. He did not seem to care what I had to say. Instead, He whispered to me again, "Go and pray with him." Left with no choice, I reluctantly obeyed and walked into the patient's room. After exchanging some pleasantries and assessing his medical condition, I proceeded with my God-dictated agenda. I asked the patient if I could pray with him. There was a long awkward pause, followed by his saying, "I'm sorry, I need to go to the bathroom." I did not take offense. In fact, I was relieved. I never wanted to do it in the first place. I quickly excused myself and thought, "I did my part, and it was not my fault he was not interested in my strange offer to pray with him." But at the back of my mind, I knew I would not be able to get away with it that easily. Shortly after I left the patient's room, I felt God nudging me to go back in and ask if I could pray with him. I had no more energy to fight with God, so I returned, went straight to the point, and told the patient I wanted to pray with him. All the while I thought, "Let's get this over with." Surprisingly, this time, he was willing and even seemed appreciative. His demeanor was different. He was calm and more relaxed. He opened up to me about his relationship with his family and friends. Basically, he had no one in his life because he had driven them away. It became clear that he was a difficult man, to which he admitted. No one wants to be alone, but I had the impression he made it impossible for the people around him not to leave, because he felt he did not deserve to be loved. I spent time listening to him and talked to him kindly. Somehow, in that moment, I truly cared about him, and I wanted him to know. I genuinely felt badly for him. Sometimes, people just cannot help how they act because they do not feel well about themselves. It may be due to their personalities, or to adverse circumstances in life that made them become who they are. I talked to him about God, and I prayed with him. I wanted him to believe that God loves him even if he did not think anybody else did. I encouraged him to get to know God more by reading the Bible. But there was one problem. There

six weeks after his hospital discharge, the following was reported: "The previously noted extensive infiltrative lesion in the right lobe of the liver and the medial segment of the left lobe of the liver appear to have regressed dramatically in the interval." Six months later, another MRI of the abdomen showed complete resolution of the liver masses. The patient lived for another seven years and seven months from the time he opened his heart to God in prayer; that night I said "yes" to God to pray with him.

CHAPTER 20
THAT'S ALL IT TAKES

Once a year, I fly overseas to the Philippines to spend time with my parents. Family and friends usually visit me whenever I am in town. On this particular year, my godmother asked to see me at my mother's house. Her son happens to be the childhood friend of mine I mentioned in chapter fifteen, who was skeptical about assigning special meanings to the butterfly sightings of his wife. My friend and his wife accompanied my godmother to visit me. We had not seen each other in a while, and this was a great opportunity for us to reacquaint. My godmother is also one of my mom's best friends, and I was sure they wanted to see each other as well. Although there was nothing unusual about the meeting, their extraordinary efforts to arrange it made me wonder what their motivation was. I somehow suspected there was something more than just wanting to get together.

After exchanging the typical pleasantries, I learned that my godmother had been sick for some time. She suffered from an unexplained pain in the left lower quadrant of her abdomen. Her appetite was poor, and she had lost significant weight as a result. It left her feeling weak and looking frail. They showed me the results of her tests and asked if I had any thoughts about what might be occurring. As a gastroenterologist this fell within my purview and expertise, so I gladly obliged. All the tests she had so far did not reveal a cause of her persistent pain. Her doctors could not determine a plausible explanation and had tried various empirical treatments that yielded no effective results. I offered some suggestions and no shortage of encouragement. It now made sense why there was a sense of urgency in my godmother's voice when she called to say she wanted to see me. Or so I thought.

There was a long awkward silence that followed. I looked around the room and no one was saying anything. It seemed an eternity. My godmother then turned to my mom and meekly explained she wanted me to pray over her. My mom was baffled, and I was shocked. I am a Christian, but my godmother is not, and my mom knew that. My thoughts were racing. How was I supposed to pray for her? How did she even get that idea? I later found out my friend had shared with her stories about my spiritual journey. But still, it was no small leap for her to go from hearing about my stories to asking me to pray over her.

My family is of Chinese descent, and culturally, it is not customary for us to freely express our personal thoughts and feelings to others. Certainly, praying for someone out loud in the presence of others is very awkward and heightens the sense of vulnerability for all involved. My mom was so uncomfortable at my godmother's request that she excused herself without saying much else.

This shifted the attention back to me. All of this caught me off guard, and I did not know what to do. But I had no choice. Not doing it was not an option. I looked at my friend straight in the eye as if to ask, "What should I do?"

Looking nervous and lacking in confidence, I approached my godmother. I laid my right hand on the left lower part of her abdomen. I kept my eyes closed as I calmed myself down and focused on feeling God's presence. No matter how hard I tried, I could not make myself pray aloud at that time. So instead, I said a silent prayer that went something like this. "Dear Lord, my godmother came here today in faith, seeking healing from you through me. She may not really know you the way I know you, but somehow, she believes that you are the one who has the power to heal her. I ask that you reward her childlike faith and deep conviction that led her to come here today. I feel this is a perfect opportunity for you Lord, to show her, her son, and her daughter-in-law, who are witnessing this right now, who you are and what you can do. I pray in Jesus's most powerful name that you relieve her of this persistent pain in her abdomen and restore her health. Thank you for giving me this opportunity to serve you. Amen."

With that, I breathed a sigh of relief. I was glad I did it. I was thankful I had the courage to do it. I knew that God heard my prayers and I hoped that it was His will that she be healed. We said our "goodbyes" to each other, and they went back home.

The next day, I went to the mall with my mom to return a pair of shoes I had previously purchased for her. The music inside was blaring and I did not realize my cellphone had been ringing, and I missed a few calls. My godmother's son had been trying to reach me. When he called again for the third time, I was able to answer. I apologized profusely and asked if everything was okay with his mother. He assured me that everything was fine, but then I wondered why he was seemingly so determined to reach me such that he called three times within a few minutes.

He asked, "Did you feel anything when you were praying for my mom?" I innocently answered, "Was I supposed to feel something?" I did not expect this phone call, and surely, I did not expect him to ask me that question. I felt uncomfortable answering, and I tried to deflect as much as I could. The truth is, I did feel something, but I was not going to tell anyone. Even I was not sure what I felt nor what it meant. I did not want to risk being ridiculed by people who do not believe in divine interventions.

He then proceeded to tell me what happened to his mother after they left my mom's house. While in the car, his mother told him she thought she was getting better. Then, at around five o'clock the next morning, she woke up and had severe abdominal cramps. She went to the bathroom and had a bowel movement. Since then, she was completely pain free. Her appetite was back, and she felt well.

I told him that while I was praying over his mom, with my right hand on her left lower abdomen, I felt something like a bag of water move under my palm. I thought it was strange. The movement was pronounced, but that was all there was. Until he had asked about it, I was intrigued by the experience, but never really gave it much thought afterwards.

My godmother has remained well ever since. She has slowly gained her weight back and returned to her usual self.

God stirs our hearts to seek Him and serve Him, because He knows this is the path to peace, contentment, and true happiness. All it takes on our part is the willingness to trust and the courage to obey.

CHAPTER 21
OVERFLOWING FAITH

One ordinary Wednesday afternoon, my nurse received an unusual, not-so-ordinary phone call. A patient of mine called and demanded an appointment for his daughter the following day at 4:30 p.m. That was an impossible request. I was usually booked weeks in advance. He wanted an appointment within twenty-four hours, and at a specific time at that. I had never encountered anyone with the audacity to make such a request. Even if someone had, I doubted there was any doctor who would be able to accommodate such a demand.

I asked my nurse who this patient was. She gave me his name and told me that his daughter would be flying in from Florida the following day, and she would like to try to make it by 4:30 p.m. at my office. I asked her what the emergency was. She told me my patient wanted to make an appointment for me to pray over his daughter. Baffled, I asked, "What?"

So, I looked up this patient's chart, as I could not readily recollect the name. Once I realized who he was, I told my nurse to go ahead and book his daughter as he had requested.

This man had the most unusual life experience. During one of his office visits, he shared that he had suffered a stroke and could not move his limbs. He was a very spiritual man who believed God would heal him. One day, his church planned a meeting to pray for his healing. He was in a wheelchair, and several of his friends gathered in a circle forming a chain to include him. They took turns praying for him, and suddenly, he felt a bolt of electricity flow through his entire body. He said he was immediately healed; he was able to move all his extremities, rose from his wheelchair, and walked like he did prior to the stroke.

This was an incredible story; one I was uncertain to believe. But why would he make it up? I could not see what he stood to gain. In a way, I understood how it was to be examined with skepticism when sharing unusual spiritual experiences like his. To reassure him I did believe in divine interventions, I shared with him some of my experiences during our daughter's illness where God made His presence known. He listened as

I told him how God sent us butterflies to remind us of His promise to heal Jaymie completely. When I told him about God anointing my hand to heal the sick, he jumped out of his chair and insisted that I lay my hand on his neck and down his spine. At that time, he was having some neck and back issues that limited his movements. It was certainly an awkward moment. He was passionate and demanded it like I owed him a fortune. And so, I did. I had never been put on the spot like that. I laid my right hand on his neck and moved it down his spine as I prayed out loud for him. The patient later indicated he felt a warm sensation travel from his neck down to his lower spine, and he felt better. Again, this is him telling me this. Only he knows if it is the truth.

The following day, my patient showed up at exactly 4:30 p.m. with his daughter. After exchanging greetings, she proceeded to tell me about her recent diagnosis of lupus. She had severe joint pains in various parts of her body. Not only was she miserable because of this, she was also anxious about her future and the prognosis of her illness. During her two-hour plane ride, she could not find a comfortable position and was exhausted from the sheer struggle. I expressed my sympathy and offered to pray with her.

The three of us sat facing each other. We held hands, and I led the prayer. I closed my eyes and prayed out loud to God. I implored Him to heal my patient's daughter, to comfort her, and to give her hope. I then paused for a second and waited for one of them to take their turn to say a prayer. A few minutes passed by, and there was complete silence. I opened my eyes and looked around. My patient looked like he was in a trance. He was swaying from left to right in a steady rhythm, with his eyes closed. He did not utter a word. His daughter sat in silence and was very still. I closed my eyes again and prayed in silence. After a while, I ran out of things to say in prayer and felt distracted and restless. I looked at my watch and realized more than an hour had elapsed. My patient was still swaying, and his daughter, as statuesque as an hour prior. They both continued holding my hands tightly. I wanted to break away from them, but I was embarrassed. They both seemed so deep in their own world. My arms were getting heavy, so I rested both of my elbows on my legs. I closed my eyes again and tried to keep praying. Somehow, I could not focus anymore. I was tired from a long day's work and from this over-extended prayer session. I made some small noises here and there trying to wake them both from their trance-like state to no avail. Suddenly, there was a knock on the door. I thought, "Thank you, Jesus!" They both let go of my hand. I was free! Unfortunately, it was not for very long. The janitor opened the door, shocked to see the three of us sitting in a circle doing nothing. He apologized profusely for disrupting us, and quickly closed the door. As soon as the door shut, both of them grabbed my hands again and went back to their trance-like state. At that point, I thought, "This

And as she looked down, another butterfly flew out from inside her shoe that laid right beside her foot.

This story, and its subplots, seem hard to believe. I was involved in some parts of it and can testify to what happened. Other parts of the story were merely told by my patient. I shared them all with you as I recall them. It was not my objective to have a scientific discussion about the plausibility of each story. I processed the events above, in my mind, at their face value. What really matters is they gave me hope. They also made God's love more real to me. This, in a sense, is what God's true purpose is when He intervenes in our lives.

Chapter 22
The Mystery of a Whisper

A *nd he said, "Go out and stand on the mount before the* Lord.*" And behold, the* Lord *passed by, and a great and strong wind tore the mountains and broke in pieces the rocks before the* Lord, *but the* Lord *was not in the wind. And after the wind an earthquake, but the* Lord *was not in the earthquake. And after the earthquake a fire, but the* Lord *was not in the fire. And after the fire the sound of a low whisper. And when Elijah heard it, he wrapped his face in his cloak and went out and stood at the entrance of the cave. And behold, there came a voice to him and said, "What are you doing here, Elijah?"* (1 Kings 19:11-13 ESV)

The intense pain I experienced as I helplessly watched our daughter suffer through her prolonged life-threatening illness, brought me closer to God. I had developed a heightened sensitivity to His subtle whispers, and I could "hear" His voice with my heart. He often nudges me to act in the most unusual and unexpected circumstances. My awareness of His presence was akin to a fish recognizing it is surrounded by water. Sensing His presence allowed me to breathe and swim. I could discern His voice because it was familiar. I had heard it many times before, and it comforted and encouraged me as I tried to rise from the weight of the agony I endured. It was always gentle. It always gave me courage and peace.

A longtime patient of mine bled from his large intestine and received seven pints of blood in two days. I was asked to see him in the hospital, and I did an emergency colonoscopy to search the source of bleeding. Despite an extensive and careful examination of the entire colon, I could not find where he bled from. As I was ready to call it quits, I experienced an unsettling, irrational feeling to re-examine the entire colon. My patient was critically ill, and I prayed for him to make it through this predicament. His life was in my hands now, but I was aware that I did not have the power to determine the ultimate outcome. Given the amount of time already elapsed performing the procedure, my staff naturally protested when I told them about my plan. They thought I was out of my mind. Nonetheless, I did it anyway. I was sure that God was directing my steps. In a situation like this, when human wisdom has reached its limits, rejecting the path of faith would be unwise.

When I got back up to the very top of the colon, called the cecum, I suddenly saw blood gushing out. The area filled up with blood quickly. I knew I had to stop the bleeding as soon as possible, or he would succumb to it. This was the opportunity I was seeking. I suctioned the blood and flushed the area aggressively. For a moment, I saw what I thought was a protruding artery, called a Dieulafoy's lesion, squirting pulsatile blood at a fast rate. I injected epinephrine in the general area where I saw the lesion. Luckily, the bleeding slowed down, and I could visualize the culprit. I placed a metal clip over the artery, and the bleeding stopped. The timing was perfect. I could not have made it happen that way. If I had missed the chance to treat this bleeding vessel, he would have continued to hemorrhage and would likely not survive. God answered my prayer, and my patient was healed. I witnessed a miracle when I abandoned what I thought was wise and placed my confidence in a voice that I could only feel.

During weekend call duties at the hospital, I would attend to an average of forty patients each day. Most of my patient encounters were ordinary and uneventful. There were a few that were unusual, and the following being one of them.

I met a patient with end-stage liver disease for the first time. She was my partner's patient, and I was just overseeing her treatment over the weekend. She was confused because her liver was not functioning optimally, causing a build-up of ammonia in her brain. At the time, she was relatively stable, despite being terminally ill due to her chronic liver failure. She did not require much treatment that day. I went about my routine of reviewing her chart, asking her a few questions, and examining her. Apart from her continually talking about having been a prostitute in the past, there was nothing exceptional about the visit. She was crying and seemed terrified. Since this volatile behavior was not unusual for someone with advanced liver failure, this presented as a straightforward case, and I assumed I would be leaving quickly.

However, every time I took a step toward the door, I felt a heaviness in my heart. It was as if I wanted to leave, yet I knew I shouldn't. I tried not to listen to her cry and scream about her past, because it bothered me. It made it difficult for me to leave the room. I had many more patients to see, and I wanted to go home and see my family. Furthermore, I did not know what I was supposed to or could do for her; I did not even know what to say to her. Hard as I tried to ignore the internal debate in my mind, I somehow just knew deep inside that I was not yet supposed to leave the room. So, I did the only thing that I knew was the right thing to do at the time; I stayed. Then I instinctively grabbed a chair and sat by the patient's bedside. I thought I might as well sit down if I had to stay longer.

I proceeded to ask her if she was okay, and she

calmed down immediately. She told me again that she was a prostitute when she was younger and added that she felt ashamed and horrified of what she did. She knew she was very sick and feared dying. As I listened to her speak, I began to understand her pain and anxiety, which moved me deeply. I suddenly found the words I needed to say, the courage to do what I believed I was called to do, and the love to open my heart to someone in desperate need. She may have been confused, but at that moment, I felt like she knew what she was telling me, and she was able to comprehend what I shared with her. I told her how much God loved her and how He had been patiently waiting for her to accept His offer of forgiveness. I prayed with her and comforted her. She seemed to be at peace when I finally left her room. That was the first and last time I saw her.

God used her sorrow to bring her back to Him and to move my heart to obey His will. Sometimes, I cannot help but wonder, "What if I had ignored God's whisper?"

Most days are ordinary, which is a good thing. Those uneventful days are devoid of the high highs and the low lows. On one such day, I walked down the hallway of the hospital mindlessly. I was unaware of time and my surroundings. Out of nowhere, I bumped into one of my patients. She seemed to want to say more than just, "Hi." She told me she was there because her brother was involved in a motor vehicular accident and was in a coma in the intensive care unit (ICU). I asked her if I could help her in any way. I tried to comfort her and promised to pray for her brother and their family. She knew that was not an empty promise and I meant it. She then asked if I would go check on her brother for her and let her know how he was doing. I was not busy at the time, and I told her I would check on him immediately.

I searched her brother's name on the ICU board and went to his bedside. I did not check his medical chart as I was not involved in his care, and it would not be proper to do so. I just stood and looked at him with the breathing tube down his throat and multiple wires and plastic tubes attached to various parts of his body. He was motionless. The beeping from the monitors consumed my senses. He was badly bruised and had bandages surrounding his head. Despite this grim view before me, I felt a bright kind of energy; I felt peace. There was a disparity between what my eyes witnessed and what I felt. Hence, the situation did not seem as dismal. I held his hand, closed my eyes, and prayed for him in silence. I returned to the family waiting room and spoke to my patient, who was anxiously waiting for my report on her brother. The first words I uttered were "He is in there." I can still remember the confused look on her face. She asked, "What do you mean?" I explained that I felt her brother was present in that lifeless body. It sounded quite unintelligent, but that was as best I could explain it. Obviously, he was alive because his heart was beating, and the ventilator was breathing on his behalf, but I had me. I would treat everyone the same, regardless of their societal stature.

Then, the man asked, "Do you really not remember me?" I politely said, "I'm sorry. I really do not remember you." He broke out in a grin and reminded me of how we met eight years prior.

He was a very sick man who had severe acute pancreatitis and was in the hospital for several weeks. His doctor was one of my partners and I had assumed his care while on call one weekend. At the time, his prognosis was not clear. His recovery was very slow, and he was losing hope. He said, I shared with him then, stories about God's faithfulness during our daughter's illness. At the end of the visit, he said I left him with these words, "You are going to live." He cherished those words, and they gave him hope. He had been praying to God for healing, strength, and encouragement, and at that moment, he felt that God heard him and answered his plea. I had no idea why I said those words, but I am glad I did. To him, those five words that I declared were what kept him alive. He came with his wife that day to personally thank me for lending God my voice to speak life into him.

It is very encouraging to hear stories like this. However, in reality, we do not always get to see the results of our obedience to God's commands.

One late night at the hospital, I walked down a hallway toward the ICU. There were benches by the hallway windows where patients' families could sit. I saw a weary old man sitting there by himself. His eyes were fixated on the floor, and he seemed oblivious to his surroundings. I felt pity for him. It was obvious to me that his heart was heavy, and his body, tired. For some reason, I was drawn to this man. I wanted to sit beside him and comfort him, but it felt awkward. It was also late, and I still had patients to see. I deliberated in my mind whether to approach him or not. This back and forth in my head continued for a while. I had already walked past this guy and still could not decide what to do. I somehow realized that I was really debating with God, and as such, I knew who was going to win. I ended my futile resistance and walked back to the man. He did not even lift his head when I sat beside him. So, I said, "How are you doing? Is there anything I can do for you?" He tried to smile and shook his head. I pressed by asking, "Have you eaten?" He nodded and said no more. I sat for a few more minutes, got up, and walked away.

I do not know what happened to the man or his sick family member. I do not understand why God tugged my heart to approach him or how my action affected him. What is important to me is knowing that I recognized God's voice and I obeyed. Hopefully, it led to something good, or even fulfilled God's bigger plans. Maybe it is better that I do not always see the outcome of my efforts. This way, I can rest assured that my motivation for obeying is solely to please God, and not to seek the reward of witnessing His wonders.

Since Jaymie's illness, I find solace spending time in prayer. I read and meditate on scripture verses, and actively seek to quiet my mind. I experience profound peace as I feel like I am resting comfortably in the embrace of a loving being. I can communicate my deepest longings to God without uttering a word, and I receive wisdom and inspiration fortuitously. Sometimes, names or faces of random people surface in my consciousness during this time. This practice has made my relationship with God grow deeper and more intimate.

On one November morning many years ago, during my prayer and meditation time, a high school classmate suddenly came to mind. I had not seen this person for many years. He lived overseas, eight thousand miles away, in the Philippines. We rode the school bus together and that was the extent of our connection. I had heard through the grapevine he had been in a coma for several years. Apparently, he woke up one day to use the bathroom and collapsed. Since then, he remained in a vegetative state. He had a major bleed in his brain which was thought to be due to a hypertensive crisis. Unexplainably, I felt a calling to fast for him. At the same time, a scripture, Matthew 18:20 kept replaying in my mind. *"For where two or three are gathered in My name, I am there in the midst of them."* I started making phone calls to mutual friends overseas, looking for at least one person to join me in this prayer and fasting mission. Eventually, I was able to find a former classmate who was willing to buy into this random and seemingly capricious idea. We offered this sacrifice to lift this person in prayer hoping for a miracle.

A month later, I experienced a similar occurrence. While deep in prayer, I felt an intense, irrational need to fly overseas and pray over the same person. It was as if his life depended on me. I was reminded of the anointing of my hand to heal the sick (discussed in chapter two), and I was convinced that I was being instructed by God to carry out His plan. I had not seen this person in almost thirty years, and I had no idea what his house looked like. With my eyes closed in prayer, I saw a vision of him lying in a hospital-type bed. There were about ten people, including myself, holding hands and standing around his bed in a circle. I recognized one or two faces in the group, but the others were vague and sort of blended with the background. The bed was positioned in the northwest corner of the room, beside a large window, and the walls were painted blue. There was no other furniture in the room; it was a peaceful scene.

I quickly searched for a reasonably priced plane ticket to fly to the Philippines. This was not an inexpensive undertaking as it was also peak season to travel to that part of the world. Nonetheless, I figured it was a worthy endeavor. Not only would I feel I had fulfilled a life purpose, but it also gave me an extra opportunity to see my parents. My father was sick, and I tried to visit him as often as possible. My mother always appreciated the company and the extra help and support I gave them.

When I reached my destination, I contacted a few friends and explained the reason behind my surprise visit. I asked if any of them would accompany me to visit and pray over our former classmate. My friend, Raymond, committed to joining me in this spiritual adventure without hesitation. A few years back, he had experienced God's incredible grace and love through the healing of his son who was born with a rare disease of the liver and bile duct, called biliary atresia. After some struggles and challenges, his infant son eventually received a liver transplant and has been doing wonderfully ever since.

I reached out to the sister of this former classmate who was comatose, and asked if Raymond and I could visit. I explained that we heard about her brother's condition through other classmates, and we were hoping we could go see and pray over him. It felt awkward at first, but when we finally met in person, it went smoother than expected, as she made us feel welcome and appreciated. After we briefly introduced ourselves, she told us what had happened to her brother and updated us on his current medical condition. It was very sad to see anyone in that state. He was very thin and appeared chronically ill. His limbs were reduced to skin and bone. They moved intermittently, but it was difficult to distinguish if the movements were purposeful or involuntary. His extremities lacked strength, but he could occasionally move some fingers on command. He did not do this consistently for us to make a conclusive determination. It appeared that he had good nursing care, as I did not see any bed sores despite years of immobility. He did not have joint contracture like many patients in similar condition do. He had somehow retained some joint flexibility. His eyes were open, but they were floating from left to right, and did not seem to have the ability to focus. There were a few times when it seemed that he may have been tracking us with his eyes. He blinked intermittently and we tried a few times to ask him if he could hear us, encouraging him to respond in the affirmative by blinking twice. Somehow, we were convinced he was able to hear us.

I brought a vial of the "healing oil" that Father Ralph gave me. I made the sign of the cross with it on his forehead, chest, and both arms and legs. His sister and caretaker joined us in praying for him. We stood around his bed, held hands, and took turns saying a prayer over him. I was consumed with emotion as we prayed. My hands and voice shook, I struggled to complete my sentences, tears flowed freely, and my shirt was soaked with sweat. The experience was surreal. It was overwhelming. God's presence in that room was undeniable. Although the physical appearance of the room was nothing like what I saw in my vision, the feeling was identical. There was a profound sense of awe that filled the hearts of those of us in that room. After we left and got into Raymond's car, he offered me an extra shirt that he brought with him. He said, "I came prepared. I knew it was going to be intense."

A few months after this spiritual adventure, I began doubting my experience. I started to debate whether God really instructed me to make that impulsive decision to fly overseas and pray over someone. Could it have been my mind playing games with me? I guess that would be what most people might say. It was so irrational that I did not even tell my family about it. They probably just presumed I wanted to see my parents. I felt foolish having done something like that.

One night, I stopped by the chapel on my way home from work to pray. I knelt and asked God to confirm, in no uncertain terms, if He truly asked me to make that trip. My hands were clasped together as I prayed intensely. I screamed silently in my mind demanding an answer from God. My hands started to feel heavy, and my fingers felt like gold bars smelted into one piece. Suddenly, I felt a pair of hands supporting mine from underneath. A sense of peace followed. I believed that I received the confirmation I needed from God.

Once a year, I visited this former classmate who remained in a vegetative state. Raymond always accompanied me to these visits. Each year, more people joined us as they learned about our "ministry." Better still, some people organized small groups of their own and visited him themselves. I helped raise the awareness that this person might be locked-in his paralyzed body and could possibly still experience a whole range of emotions. If this were true, the loneliness and isolation he may feel would be unimaginable. I tried to encourage the people who were within my scope of influence to share their time with him. When his mother was still alive, she read him the newspaper daily. I am thankful that he still has his sister and some loving caretakers. Many are helping provide for his medical and nutritional needs. Hopefully, many will also give the gift of time to help ease his unfathomable pain of loneliness.

I was called to pray over him. I anointed him with the "healing oil." We hoped for a miracle. It had been years since I made that radical decision to obey what I believed was God's prompting. Nothing has changed in this person's condition. Could it be that the miracle we were seeking was the transformation of our hearts? To have a heart that can feel other people's pain? To have the courage to speak for those who cannot? And to fight for those who have no strength to do so on their own?

CHAPTER 23
THE CERTAINTY OF SUNRISE

Throughout this journey with Jaymie, we dealt with crises as they came; there were so many of them, we could only focus on what was in front of us. The present was so overwhelming that we could not even wonder about the future. Each day was a struggle, and we fought hard to make it to another day. All that mattered each time, was the immediate battle confronting us. We believed if we could only survive each one that comes our way, we would eventually make it to the other side. There, the sun shines brightly, and darkness cannot co-exist. There was certainly no guarantee about winning this battle, but we had faith that one way or another, all would be well. The messages and messengers God sent us helped provide the resilience and hope we needed, as we patiently waited for the dawn of a new day.

When life is going well and we feel in control, it is hard to accept how things can suddenly go very wrong. Our experiences revealed to us how unpredictable life could be. God had power over our situation, and yet, He allowed bad things to happen. We blamed Him for all our misery. Bitterness then started to take root, and our pain worsened. Fortunately, we realized over time, that God, the author of our agony, actually cared deeply about us. We then started to ask ourselves, "What could have been the purpose of all this?" This was the beginning of our path to enlightenment. We began to enjoy peace amidst chaos and uncertainty.

We rode an emotional roller coaster as we went through a series of incorrect diagnoses, and consequently, ineffective treatment. The doctors did their best with the knowledge they had and the information available to them. This perpetuated for a while, and it took a toll on us. We could not hope for a cure because we had yet to figure out what the disease was. How could they treat a disease they could not identify? Every time a doctor proposed a plausible explanation of Jaymie's illness, we followed a specific treatment plan until it proved unsuccessful, or it became apparent that the working diagnosis was incorrect. We went through this vicious cycle several times over. Meanwhile, Jaymie's condition worsened, and we became more discouraged and desperate. As time elapsed, God lined up perfectly the right people and unique circumstances that led to figuring out the correct diagnosis and treatment. The journey to this point was long, but God provided us all that we needed. He also used these experiences to open our eyes to the truth about ourselves, Him, and the people around us. We learned how to trust Him and wait patiently for His loving plan to manifest in His perfect time. Through this process, we resisted and rebelled, but it became obvious that even that was part of God's plan. We were more resolute in submitting to God's will, once we learned from the follies of our resistance and rebellion. While we were in the dark searching for the diagnosis of Jaymie's illness, it felt like it would never end. But once the waiting had served God's purpose, the doctors were finally able to make a firm diagnosis. Although we knew there were formidable days ahead, we at least had hope. Hope that the available treatment would lead to a cure. The doctors warned us that the treatment could be worse than the disease. Jaymie's disease was rare, and reports on its treatment outcomes were scant. There were a lot of uncertainties but there was no question that our options were limited, and time was running out. We needed to be decisive and take our chances. This time, however, something was different. We made a paradigm shift and took our chances in letting God fight our battles and leave the outcome in His hands. Instead of frantically seeking answers that often were not there, we decided to seek God's promptings and did what He led us to do. In fact, we made a pledge as a family, and Jaymie created a poster that we displayed on her hospital room door to help remind us of it each day. It read, "Our Daily to carry on and lend meaning to our suffering. Most importantly, it gave us hope that we would be alright, no matter what the outcome might be.

A few years before Jaymie got sick, my father developed Parkinson's-like symptoms and later had a stroke. His health progressively declined, culminating to the point he was unable to communicate and was fed through a feeding tube inserted into his stomach. He was paralyzed and only had short periods of time when he opened his eyes and appeared to have limited awareness of his surroundings. He lived overseas, and I visited him and my mom as often as I could. My mother needed help and support through those difficult times, and I tried to be there for her. When Jaymie got sick, I could not leave her, and I could not see my parents for almost an entire year. I called my mom frequently to keep her company and give advice when needed. One morning, during one of our routine calls, she told me she had to bring my father to the hospital the night before, as he was not doing well. In the middle of our conversation, she frantically told me she had to end the call as my dad had stopped breathing. A few hours later, he passed away.

As this was all happening, my wife was with Jaymie at her routine follow-up appointment with the doctor. The visits always took a long time. They drew blood at the beginning of the visits, followed by the doctor asking questions and examining Jaymie. My wife would then anxiously wait for the blood test results and the doctor's treatment recommendations. I would be at work and constantly checking in with my wife to find out about the outcome of the visit; I was always anxious born out of receiving so much bad news from past visits. But this day was different. The doctor reviewed the blood test results with my wife. Jaymie's blood counts had been stable for a reasonable span of time now and her disease markers had stayed normal. He recommended the PICC line on Jaymie's arm, through which she received blood transfusions and had her blood drawn, could finally be removed. In essence, after a long and arduous course, he declared that Jaymie was disease-free.

On that remarkable and miraculous January day, my dad went to be with the Lord and relieved of all his sufferings, Jaymie was cured after a long and hard battle, and God blessed me with another birthday.

There are not many things in life we can be certain of each day. But one thing we can always count on, is that no matter how dark the night may be, in a few hours, the sun will always rise.

CHAPTER 24

REFLECTIONS OF A
HUMBLED HEART

Hurts, disappointments, losses, failures, and sufferings are powerful tools God can use to accomplish His purpose. They can prepare us to serve Him or prime us to receive the blessings He has in store for us. They can rebuke, release shackles, or lead us away from disaster and toward the promised life of bliss. When faced with afflictions, we tend to question why they happen to us. In these situations, we should consider asking God what His purpose might be for allowing them. Or maybe, try to discern what message He might be wanting to impart. As the cascade of unfortunate events unfold, our tendency is to resist. We blame ourselves or others for them. We constantly live in regret and dwell on what could have been or why the things that must be are not. Arguing why the unfortunate events should not have transpired is an exercise in futility. It fools us into believing that we are fighting, and not simply, giving up. I have come to realize that resisting does not soothe or alleviate the pain. If anything, the resistance drains our limited energy. Energy we could be channeling to something more productive. As I mature in my faith in God, I am beginning to be open to just letting life play itself out. Life will progress regardless, despite my feelings surrounding it. Refusing to resist is not a passive acceptance of the inevitable. Rather, it is an active process of allowing us to experience life and participate in its complexities and nuances. We let ourselves feel the different layers of emotions that it includes, and we interact with it. We ride the waves of emotions and yet, be careful not to let them control us. It is important to identify the emotions as separate from ourselves, and we become mere observers of them. They are an external energy that happen to flow through us at a particular moment in time. Unless we decide to hold on to them, they should eventually pass through like a storm. In this process of embracing life and actively experiencing it, we feel, we watch, and we act, only when necessary. As we walk through the dark and cold valley of the unknown, we should focus on simply putting one foot in front of the other, one moment at a time. We should wait patiently for our deliverance from the pain, resting in the assurance that God will provide the strength, guidance, and wisdom as we climb this rocky road.

I have come to realize that I am always better off letting God be God. I do not know enough to know what is good for me. I also do not want to limit what God can do for me by limiting my prayers to what my finite mind can imagine. In Isaiah 55:8 NIV, the Lord declares *"For my thoughts are not your thoughts, neither are your ways my ways."* My eyes have seen miracles, born of the love God has for us, when He answered our prayers. He delivered those gifts in the most unexpected ways and He gave us more than we could have ever thought to ask. He blessed us when we had done nothing to deserve them. He even blessed us when we had done things that made us undeserving. I was in awe of God when He answered my prayers, even when that response was, "no" or "wait." I may have felt rejected, betrayed, or abandoned by Him at the time, but He eventually opened my eyes; I saw how He protected me from myself, taught me to be patient, and showed me the satisfaction of trusting Him. I agreed to surrender my life and submit my will to Him because I trust Him. I believe that He will supply all my needs at the opportune time, and I am confident that He will always look out for my best interest. My job is to pray, and God's job is to make things happen. How He decides to do it and whatever the outcome may be, I will choose to believe that in the end, all will be well.

We, as Christians, know that Jesus suffered and died in the most gruesome way for our sins. However, many of us only understand this on an intellectual and impersonal level. I, myself, had not truly felt the emotional impact of someone giving up his comfort and life for my sake until our daughter fell ill. Jaymie, at the tender age of five, suffered tremendously both physically and emotionally. Her body was ravaged by the disease and the treatment. She lost a lot of her hair during chemotherapy and grew unwanted hair on her face and extremities. Her body was disfigured due to muscle wasting from malnutrition and the catabolic effects of her disease. She withstood mental anguish from her prolonged confinement in the hospital and the constant threat of pain from endless needlesticks and invasive procedures. These contributed to her sense of loneliness, isolation, shame, and helplessness. My wife and I had a lot of difficulty coping with Jaymie's illness. It was tough to watch her suffer and find ourselves unable to assist. The dearth of information about her disease, limited treatment options, and the uncertainty of her prognosis made us very anxious and many times, left us feeling hopeless. No matter how much we think we understood Jaymie's pain, I'm sure that the reality is nowhere close. Certainly, the pain we experienced was also but a fraction of what she had to endure. Nevertheless, after several months of living in a pressure cooker dealing with the ups and downs of Jaymie's illness, the way I see and interpret life have changed. In a way, it was like the rough and uneven surfaces I had were polished by a metal scrub or sandpaper. Even though it hurt significantly, and I was figuratively bleeding, I could see the luster underneath starting to emerge. Certain things that used to bother or annoy me gradually ceased to affect me in the same way. I was less easily angered and became more forgiving. There were habits I never thought I could surrender for which I suddenly found myself losing the desire. A lot of this had to do with knowing that God had been so good to my family and me, and all I wanted was to do what pleases Him. As I walked with God through our sufferings, I learned to trust Him, and I came to believe that He loved me. As a result, I accepted His outstretched hand that had been waiting to rescue me from that which was ensnaring me. Inspired by this, I sketched a person standing behind the iron bars of a prison cell, door wide open, with one foot outside. That image represented what I felt and how I saw myself. God opened the prison door for me, and yet, I chose to remain inside. This journey with our daughter made me take that step out and reached for the hand of God. Subsequently, it was no longer enough for me to be content with just avoiding sin and not hurting others. I found a higher purpose for my life, and I started to proactively seek people to love and help. I realized Jaymie had to suffer to save me from the progressive decline in my spiritual life, which would undoubtedly lead to self-destruction in a matter of time. God knew what it would take to get my attention. I am forever grateful to my daughter for letting God use her in this way. I am very thankful that she gave up her comfort for a prolonged period for my sake. Watching my beloved five-year-old child suffer on my behalf, made me understand what Jesus had done for me. It writing a book about my spiritual journey, so he said, "No wonder the devil is throwing all these things at you. He is trying to stop you from finishing this book." At that moment, it was like a fire was lit under me, and I felt this intense motivation to keep writing and take it to the finish line. Realizing the malicious intent of the devil gave me the extra push to overcome any hurdles he put ahead of me to keep me from achieving my goal. Over the past eight months, I wrote fourteen chapters, and I am now finishing up the last few paragraphs of this final chapter.

In the gospel (Luke 18:35-43 NIV), Jesus healed a blind beggar on his way to Jericho. The man called out, "Jesus, Son of David, have mercy on me!" When Jesus asked what he wanted Him to do, the man said, "Lord, I want to see." Jesus said to him, "Receive your sight; your faith has healed you." After that, the beggar "immediately received his sight and followed Jesus, praising God. When all the people saw it, they also praised God."

I was the beggar, spiritually blind and poor. God showed me mercy and healed me through my daughter's illness. He loved me both for, and in spite of, who I was. I felt accepted, forgiven, and secure. Over time, I gradually learned to love myself, let go of past hurts, allow myself to make mistakes, and forgive myself. As a result, I found peace. This does not mean that I never experience turbulence anymore; they just do not last as long because I do not see a reason to let it. Having experienced God's unconditional love, I developed a deep desire to please Him. I am still human and succumb to sin, but I have a heightened awareness of the ugly face of sin and the lies of the devil. My longing for God has become stronger than my need for the temporary pleasures of sin. I have also seen the pure joy and satisfaction of living a life aligned with God's will. This, in and of itself, enlightened me and helped me make better choices between good and evil. Like the blind beggar in the gospel, after I received my sight, I decided to live my life, as best as I can, in obedience to God's will. He loved me first and I want to reciprocate that love by doing what pleases Him. What pleases God is for us to love one another as He has loved us. I would like to let the whole world know what God has done for me and my family. My hope is to achieve that with this book. It is my wish that you find hope and joy as you read about God's power and goodness which he displayed during the most difficult time of our lives.

Summary

This book chronicles the ordeal the author and his family went through when their five-year-old daughter became ill with a rare and life-threatening disease. Raw in its honesty, the author shares the pain and suffering he and his family endured, the accompanying spiritual journey and transformation, and the stories of the people whose lives were touched by theirs. Fr. Ralph Jones foretold the writing of this book ten years prior. It is interesting to follow the metamorphosis of a tragedy into a glorious testimony of God's perfect will. Hopefully, this poignant and deeply personal story will fulfill its purpose to help its readers understand God's love, faithfulness, and power, and ultimately, inspire a sense of hope no matter the circumstances.

"I was in awe of God when He answered my prayers, even when that response was, "no" or "wait." I may have felt rejected, betrayed, or abandoned by Him at the time, but He eventually opened my eyes; I saw how He protected me from myself, taught me to be patient, and showed me the satisfaction of trusting Him." – TERENCE ANGTUACO, from Divine Intervention

Book Reviews

"God used this book to speak directly to my grief-stricken heart. It is an easy read that provokes deep emotions and helps initiate healing. A must-read for anyone who has ever asked, "Where are you, God?""

– Lauri Wolfe, Medical Assistant

"A touching story about a father's inspiring devotion to his family through trials and triumphs. The author shares a heart-wrenching glimpse of his personal journey and lessons in faith, obedience and perseverance. An incredible story of resiliency and must-read!"

– Allison Bermudez, Communications Consultant

"This book is a page-turner. I was quickly drawn into the story from the very beginning, as the emotions and struggles of the author were palpable. It is well written and easy to read. Witnessing how God worked in the author's life, helped me find peace in my daily trials. There is no doubt, reading this book had re-ignited my faith in God."

– Gail Erwin, Nursing Administrator

About the Author

Terence Angtuaco, a Doctor of Medicine specializing in Gastroenterology and Hepatology, practices at Premier Gastroenterology Associates in Little Rock, Arkansas. Although this is his first published book, Dr. Angtuaco has written and published several scholarly articles in his medical specialty, and also enjoys writing poetry. He likes to write and speak about the insights and wisdom he has gained from his personal struggles and victories. Dr.

Angtuaco is married and has three children and is an avid martial artist and tennis player.

www.TerenceAngtuacoMD.com

: Terence Angtuaco Writes

: terenceangtuacowrites

: Terence Angtuaco Writes

: Terence Angtuaco

Printed in the United States
by Baker & Taylor Publisher Services